INTELLIGENT COMMODITY INDEXING

INTELLIGENT COMMODITY INDEXING

A PRACTICAL GUIDE TO INVESTING IN COMMODITIES

Robert J. Greer,
Nic Johnson, Mihir P. Worah

New York   Chicago   San Francisco   Lisbon   London
Madrid   Mexico City   Milan   New Delhi   San Juan
Seoul   Singapore   Sydney   Toronto

1 2 3 4 5 6 7 8 9 10   DOC/DOC   1 8 7 6 5 4 3 2

ISBN   978-0-07-176314-1
MHID   0-07-176314-7

e-ISBN 978-0-07-176315-8
e-MHID   0-07-176315-5

This publication is designed to provide accurate and authoritative information in regard to the subject matter covered. It is sold with the understanding that neither the authors nor the publisher is engaged in rendering legal, accounting, securities trading, or other professional services. If legal advice or other expert assistance is required, the services of a competent professional person should be sought.
    —*From a Declaration of Principles Jointly Adopted by a Committee of the American Bar Association and a Committee of Publishers and Associations*

Library of Congress Cataloging-in-Publication Data

Greer, Robert J.
    Intelligent commodity indexing: a practical guide to investing in commodities / by Robert Greer, Nic Johnson and Mihir Worah.
        p. cm.
    Includes index.
    ISBN-13: 978-0-07-176314-1 (alk. paper)
    ISBN-10: 0-07-176314-7 (alk. paper)
    1. Commodity futures.   2. Investments.   3. Stock price indexes.   I. Johnson, Nic.   II. Worah, Mihir.   III. Title.
    HG6046.G74 2013
    332.64'4—dc23   2012025350

Contents

Foreword

Commodities are a relatively unexplored asset class in academia and indeed the financial markets themselves. While commodity futures have long been used by producers to hedge crops and future production, their valuation relative to "spot" prices has been only lightly explored. When PIMCO initially entered the "financial" futures markets in the early 1980s, we ordered T-shirts that trumpeted "Come with PIMCO into the Futures," and shortly thereafter we and a small group of clients were off and running on a very rewarding 30-year journey. Our research and discussions helped give us an advantage compared to competitors who were glued to the world of cash securities that in many cases were still kept in a vault. Financial innovation was PIMCO's trademark, but at the same time we made sure to walk a steady path and be wary of the inevitable derivatives quicksand.

Now, PIMCO portfolio managers Mihir Worah and Nic Johnson, along with product manager Bob Greer are continuing that journey with their book *Intelligent Commodity Indexing*. Responsible for one of the world's largest commodity practices, they are in the unique position to explain what makes for value in commodity futures and to discuss their vision on the future of commodity index investing, essentially a newer, smarter "PIMCO Index."

Principles that we at PIMCO have applied to financial futures have been and are now being applied by our commodity desk. In the following chapters you will hopefully discover a world of "carry" and "roll yield" that comes almost directly from our management of bonds and bond futures. You will read about substitution effects and their influence in terms of contract pricing. Throughout, the authors reinforce the attractiveness of commodities as an asset class, which can be used as a hedge against what PIMCO expects to be an inflationary future.

I welcome, and take pride in, the following research provided by this team of veteran PIMCO portfolio managers and hope that you as well can benefit from their thinking as we do every day on the PIMCO trading floor.

—Bill Gross, PIMCO Founder and
Co-Chief Investment Officer

Introduction

Commodities are a mainstream asset class, used by institutional investors and individual investors alike. This is a major change from just 35 years ago. Whereas stocks and bonds have been considered acceptable, at times even conservative, investments for centuries, commodities—or more specifically, commodity futures—only began to attain that status recently. Previously commodity futures markets were primarily used by commercial parties, who were looking for ways to hedge price risk. Indeed, that hedging function is the reason commodity futures markets developed in the first place. Historically that risk was assumed by speculators, who in fact were in the markets to make a profit by guessing the direction of price movements, often using leverage and giving the futures markets the reputation of being extremely risky.

Relatively recently, investors began to understand that these markets offered opportunities for inflation hedging and diversification as well as the potential for meaningful returns. Those benefits especially began to be appreciated after the stock market decline that began in 2000. As investors were drawn to this asset class, they needed a way to define just what "commodity investment" was. Like every asset class, commodities needed an investable index. There had been for many, many decades various measures of cash commodity prices, but investors now weren't typically buying cash commodities—they were buying commodity futures.

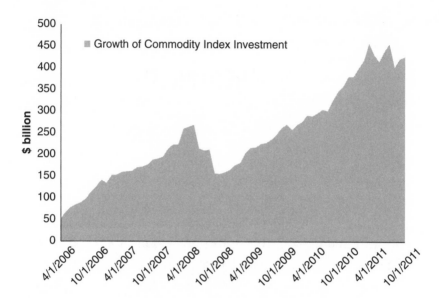

Exhibit I-1 **Growth of Commodity Index Investment**

Source: Barclays

The investment industry accommodated this need for an index of investable futures with a variety of products. And investors, using the returns of these indexes as part of their rationale for allocating to the asset class, began to commit increasing amounts of money to commodities—estimated by Barclays Capital at over $300 billion by 2010 and even higher in 2011, as shown in Exhibit I-1.

Because the development of this asset class was recent and rapid, investors did not have the wealth of underlying knowledge like that associated with stocks and bonds. They were able to evaluate the construction of commodity indexes and the historical returns of those indexes, but many investors did not have a deep appreciation for how they might intelligently use those indexes to attempt to achieve better returns than simply duplicating the calculated index. That is the reason we have written this book.

We believe investors should understand the benefits they are seeking when they approach this asset class—and understand that diversification and inflation hedging are the primary potential benefits. We believe investors should understand the historical drivers of returns achieved by commodity indexes, since as an asset class, commodities are fundamentally different from stocks and bonds. And most of all, we believe that the intelligent commodity index investor should understand how it may be possible to achieve returns that are more attractive than a calculated and published index, while retaining the fundamental benefits just mentioned. Note throughout this book, when we refer to an indexer or a commodity index investor, we are referring to an investor who is seeking to track the returns measured by a commodity index.

We have organized the book in the following sequence:

- For perspective we define commodity indexes more precisely and describe their historical development.
- Next we explain the drivers of return to this asset class and show how those drivers inherently offer the potential for inflation hedging and portfolio diversification.
- The next several chapters explain the many strategies that an intelligent commodity index investor might pursue in an attempt to achieve returns that could be more attractive than the simple calculated index, giving specific examples. These strategies include a discussion of portfolio management and risk control.
- We also include a chapter discussing many of the sources of fundamental economic data that will help a commodity investor better understand the markets.
- We then conclude with a look to the future.

As professionals in the investment management industry, we want to bring a deeper understanding to investors of how they can utilize this important asset class in their portfolios. We hope that you, as a reader, will conclude that we have done so.

INTELLIGENT COMMODITY INDEXING

CHAPTER 1

History of Commodity Indexing

There has been an interest in commodity prices, and indexes of those prices, for a very long time. Until the late 1970s, those indexes typically referred to prices of physical commodities. Part of the reason is that the interest in commodity prices stemmed from the impact that commodities had on the overall economy, whether in the United States or elsewhere. Commodities were not typically viewed as an investment vehicle in their own right.

Some of those early indexes were published by Reuters, by the *Financial Times*, by the *Economist*, and by other data sources. These indexes comprised a broad range of commodities, including commodities for which there were futures markets as well as commodities that had no futures equivalent. There were, and are, a variety of other indexes of cash commodity prices for specific industries, including livestock, energy products, and mining products. Both Dow Jones and the Commodity Research Bureau also published indexes that used the current, or spot, month of commodity futures markets as a surrogate for cash markets, partly because this information was readily available. But like those other early indexes, these published indexes based on futures prices were not investable because they could not be replicated by a financial investor. Therefore if investors wanted exposure to commodity prices, they typically would purchase the capital asset that was used to produce the commodity—farmland, or a metals mine, or an oil and gas partnership, or natural resources companies. These investments could provide some positive exposure to commodity prices, but there were drawbacks.

While the most obvious problem was liquidity, an investment in the means of producing a commodity also gave exposure to other risks, not all of which were related to commodity prices. For instance, the success of a farmland investment might depend not just on the price of the food it produced but also on the weather. And the purchase of a natural resources stock exposed the investor to the financial structure of the company and to the management talent of the company. There could also be risks unassociated with the price of the commodity, as investors in BP realized when that company's oil rig exploded in the Gulf of Mexico in 2010. In this case, while oil prices initially spiked higher due to the loss of production, BP stock actually declined significantly on anticipation of liability and cleanup costs associated with the explosion.

Actually purchasing and storing a commodity in order to benefit from an increase in its price was also typically not practical, with the exception of precious metals, for which the storage cost was small relative to the value of the investment. Industrial metals might also be purchased and stored for long periods, but in this case the storage cost was a much higher percentage of the investment. Additionally, some agricultural commodities could be purchased and stored for limited periods of time, but that type of investment would suffer from spoilage as well as from high costs for storage and insurance. Furthermore, there was not a large incentive to hold commodities in order to benefit from rising prices, since the prices of many commodities had not even kept up with inflation during the decades following World War II. This was partially the result of improving technology that enhanced extraction rates for oil and metals as well as increased yields for grains, resulting in periods when commodity supply, both actual and potential, was well above demand.

During the inflation and related shortages of several commodities, such as grains and industrial metals, in the 1970s, however, the interest in commodities for investment began to take root. But still, that interest tended to express itself in the purchase of the capital assets that actually produced commodities. Although the impact of higher commodity prices on inflation may have been well understood, the possibility of hedging against this via a systematic investment in a basket of commodity futures was generally not appreciated. Investors were typically not able to get exposure to anything like a broad-based index of commodity prices.

THE FIRST INVESTABLE COMMODITY INDEX

The early 1970s was also a time when investors first saw the idea of an investment designed to replicate an index of the stock market. Sure, there had been stock indexes for many, many years, but the first stock index fund was not offered until the early 1970s. Seeing that commodities were contributing to inflation in the 1970s, and seeing also the appearance of an investable stock index fund, gave Bob Greer the idea of finding a way for a financial investor to gain exposure to commodity prices. At that time, commodities were thought of as high-risk investments. But in fact, the price of an individual commodity may often be no more volatile than the price of a single stock. The price of wheat was typically no more volatile than the price of IBM.

There were two reasons why commodities were thought of as being so risky. The first reason was that participants in the commodity futures markets typically used a large amount of leverage. This leverage was possible because the market participants did not actually own a physical commodity, which would have required borrowed money to finance. Instead, the market participants made a commitment to buy (or sell) a commodity in the future. As long as they closed their position before they were contractually obligated to take delivery of (or deliver) the physical commodity, they only had to deposit sufficient margin to ensure that they could perform on that future commitment, adjusting that margin as the price of the future commitment moved for, or against, them. This allowed the market participants to be exposed to a large notional amount of the commodity with only a small capital commitment. Hence small adverse movements in the price of commodities could entirely wipe out the capital of these levered investors, just as small favorable moves might multiply the investors' capital manyfold. This margin deposit might be thought of as being similar to the earnest money deposit that is typically made by a buyer of a house when that house is put under contract. The full amount of the purchase price is only required when the sale is consummated. This leads to the second reason that commodity investment was misunderstood. Many investors did not understand the very nature of a futures contract. They equated having a long position in a commodity futures market with outright ownership of the commodity itself.

To take the risk of leverage out of a commodity investment, it was possible to fully collateralize the commodity contract. That is, if a live cattle contract (40,000 pounds) were trading at 50 cents per pound, the notional value of the contract would be $20,000. Instead of making a minimum margin deposit of, say, $1,000, investors could allocate a full $20,000 of their portfolio to support a single long contract in cattle. The investors thus would have the capital actually to purchase the cattle if these investors chose to do so. The notion of leverage is removed, because no matter how low the price of cattle might fall, the investors would have money to meet any margin call. And the investors' total return would be the return on collateral plus or minus the change in the price of the futures contract. This idea meant that the investors would always have positive exposure to a rising cattle price. It also meant that full collateralization could only take place with long positions—you can't determine how much collateral would be required to support a short position, since there is no way of knowing the maximum size of a move against you.

This type of investment also had an advantage compared with equities. The price of the asset could not go to zero; companies can go bankrupt, but cattle can't. Even in the 1956 debacle in the onion futures market, the price of the futures contract did not go to zero. (It went to 10 cents, which was less than the cost of the bags in which the onions were stored.)

Next, Greer had to determine what collateral an investor might use. He chose the 90-day bank CD rate, since he wanted to simulate a high-quality investment that typically had little noticeable interest rate risk. In most modern published indexes, the collateral is assumed to be the 30-day T-bill rate (reset weekly), since index providers want to use relatively low-risk collateral that will not unintentionally bring other financial risks into the portfolio. In addition to being low risk, T-bills can also be used as margin collateral against the underlying futures positions that make up the index. Therefore, choosing T-bills would allow the published commodity indexes to be simply replicated. However, investors have found that in an ultralow interest rate era like 2009–2011, T-bills are often thought of not only as the "risk-free" investment but also as virtually a "return-free" investment. (How investors deal with the selection of collateral is discussed in Chapter 10, "Implementation.") Thus we have the first of what are now understood to be the three defining characteristics of a commodity index: full collateralization of commodity futures positions to avoid leverage, along with a choice for what this collateral would be.

But what would happen when the commodity futures contract matured? Would the long-only investors end up taking delivery of a load of cattle? Sure, they had enough money to pay for it, since they were fully collateralized. But that's not what typical investors wanted. This problem could be overcome by rolling their position forward before the delivery date. That is, before the first delivery day for the October contract, the investors would sell the October contract and buy a December contract. The investors still maintain exposure to the rising price of cattle, but they would never actually own the cattle. In addition, they would always be earning interest on their collateral.

With this insight, Greer defined the second of the three defining characteristics of a commodity index: there would be well-defined rules for rolling the commodity futures so that investors had continuous exposure to the commodity markets without actually taking delivery or storing the physical commodities.

Investors who were worried about inflation would likely not want exposure only to cattle prices. They would want exposure to a broad-based set of commodities to get more thorough and diversified price exposure. To get this type of exposure, the investment process would have to allocate to many commodities that had sufficiently liquid futures markets, and it would have to be based on some measure of relative economic importance, such as relative importance in world trade or relative importance in a measure of inflation like the consumer price index (CPI).

Indexes today have a variety of ways of determining this relative importance, in some cases using online databases and complicated calculations. But Greer's work was before the era of personal computers and the Internet, so that the very concept of "online" did not exit. However, there were other measures to determine relative importance, two of which were the CPI published by the U.S. Department of Labor and the Reuters-U.K. price index, which weighted commodities based on their importance in world trade. Greer used these two indexes as the measure of relative importance. He first determined which commodities were represented by available futures contracts. He then lined up all the components of the Reuters-U.K. price index and mapped each component onto one of those available futures contracts. Clearly there was not an active futures market for each component of the price index, and so some improvisation was required. Greer next did the same thing with the CPI, mapping each component of the CPI against one of those limited number of available futures contracts. Here even more improvisation was required, since there was no clear way that the services component of the CPI might relate to a commodity like wheat or live hogs. The final step was to take the average of the mapping results for the two indexes to yield weights of an investable commodity index that would total to 100%. This resulted in the third criterion needed to define a commodity index: a systematic way to determine the choice of commodities to include and the relative weights among them. The first investable commodity index had been created! By "investable," as described in the introduction to this book, we mean that a financial investor might be able to replicate the returns measured by the index.

Finally, with the index methodology fully defined, Greer calculated historical results, from 1960 to 1974 (later extending the returns through 1978). Because personal computers had not yet been invented, the gathering of data and the calculation of returns were quite laborious. So Greer, after gathering data by hand from microfilmed copies of the *Wall Street Journal*, chose to calculate the index returns at six-month intervals. This meant that positions rolled forward twice a year. And because he assigned a percentage weight to each commodity, that first index rebalanced twice a year.

The results were published in the summer 1978 edition of the *Journal of Portfolio Management*. Reflecting the purpose of the index, the title of the article was "Conservative Commodities: A Key Inflation Hedge." Investable indexes today typically incorporate the principles established by that initial work. An investable commodity index should reflect the returns from an investment process that:

- Reflects the result of holding only long positions and rolling them forward according to specific rules
- Assumes all futures positions are fully collateralized
- Assumes that weighting in some fashion typically reflects the relative economic importance of components
- Follows a transparent and fully specified method of calculation

There was some additional academic research on commodity index investing in the 1980s including work by Bodie, Rosansky, and others. But there was virtually no serious investor interest. There was as yet no mechanism, like a commodity mutual fund, that would enable individual investors to get commodity index exposure. Institutional investors showed little interest, likely because either they did not understand the nature of futures contracts, much less this novel idea of indexing; or they were simply enamored by the stocks in their portfolios; or they were afraid to venture into an area where no institutions had yet invested.

THE 1990s

It was only in 1991, 13 years after Greer's pioneering work defining the first investable commodity index, that the industry saw the first commercially available index supported by a major institution. With great fanfare, Goldman Sachs announced the Goldman Sachs Commodity Index (GSCI), which is currently the most referenced commodity index, with an estimated $100 billion in assets benchmarked to it (as of December 31, 2011, estimated by Standard & Poor's). The primary motivation for this index creation was to allow investors a potential way to take advantage of commodity producers selling in the futures markets in order to hedge their product prices (discussed in Chapter 2, where we talk about the drivers of return to an index). This investment method would be intended to give investors exposure to commodities as an asset class, while improving liquidity in the markets by having a better match between buyers and sellers. Goldman later sold its index business to Standard & Poor's, so that index is now known as the S&P GSCI.

In 1993 the influential Frank Russell consulting firm published a white paper by Ernie Ankrim and Chris Hensel which explained the potential benefits of commodity indexes in an overall portfolio. The GSCI was followed by indexes supported by other investment banks in the 1990s. Bankers Trust began marketing the Bankers Trust Commodity Index (BTCI). Merrill Lynch began marketing the Merrill Lynch Energy and Metals Index (ENMET). J.P. Morgan started publishing the JPMorgan Commodity Index (JPMCI). And Daiwa Securities worked with Bob Greer to resurrect his original index, refined to become the Daiwa Physical Commodity Index (DPCI). These index providers mainly sought institutional investors, who might enter into OTC swaps to get exposure to their particular index.

Then, in 1998, the industry saw the first vehicle by which individual investors could get commodity index exposure. The Oppenheimer Funds launched the Oppenheimer Real Asset Fund, which was benchmarked to the GSCI and used structured notes to get commodity exposure. At about the same time that Oppenheimer was launching its fund, a closed-end fund was launched in the United Kingdom to track the GSCI. Oppenheimer's fund is still in existence. However, some of the shareholders of the U.K. closed-end fund forced a liquidation before the end of the century since it was trading at a discount to fair value.

There still seemed to be little interest in, or understanding of, commodity indexes. This did not, however, deter AIG from coming to market in 1997 with its own version of a commodity index, the AIGCI, which is currently the second most widely used commodity index, with an estimated $80 billion in assets benchmarked to it (estimated by Dow Jones as of June 30, 2011). The motivation behind the AIGCI was to construct an index with a weighting methodology that resulted in more intercommodity diversification than the GSCI had. It also held its position slightly further out on the forward curve, and it rebalanced once a year, while the GSCI never rebalanced based on changes in prices. Later, after aligning with Dow Jones as the calculation agent for that index in 1998, AIG renamed the index the DJAIGCI. That index was sold to UBS after AIG's downfall, and it is now offered as the DJUBSCI. Meanwhile Daiwa sold the DPCI to Chase Manhattan Bank (later merged with J.P. Morgan), where it became first the Chase Physical Commodity Index and then the JPMorgan Commodity Futures Index. J.P. Morgan quit calculating that index in 2000, and Credit Suisse eventually utilized Greer's methodology to bring to market the Credit Suisse Commodity Benchmark (CSCB) index in 2009. The defining characteristics of these three major commodity indexes are shown in Exhibit 1-1.

	DJUBSCI*	CSCB†	S&P GSCI‡
Weighting Methodology	1/3 world production value and 2/3 market liquidity	World production value with market liquidity inclusion thresholds	World production quantity with market liquidity inclusion thresholds
Contracts Used	Front month	First 3 months (equally weighted by units)	Front month
Roll Period	5 business days (fifth business day of the month to the ninth business day of the month)	15 business days (fifth business day prior to end of previous month to ninth business day of the month)	5 business days (fifth business day of the month to the ninth business day of the month)
Rebalancing Frequency	Annual	Monthly	Does not rebalance based on changes in prices
Index Reconstitution	Annual	Annual	Annual
Weighting Constraints	Seven commodity groups: max 33%§ Single commodity: max 15%, min 2%§ Single commodity and its derivatives: max 25%§	None	None

Exhibit 1-1 Defining Characteristics of the Three Major Commodity Indexes

* Dow Jones–UBS Commodity Index

† Credit Suisse Commodity Benchmark

‡ S&P Goldman Sachs Commodity Index

§ Effective at the beginning of the year when new weights are set. Actual weights may exceed during the year due to price movements.

Source: Various index providers

GROWTH IN INDEX INVESTMENT

The late 1990s saw a fair amount of research on the rationale for why commodities are a separate asset class, distinct from stocks and bonds. Stocks and bonds are both capital assets, which generate a stream of cash flow and which can be valued using net present value analysis. Commodities, while investable, don't generate a stream of cash flows. Their value derives from the fact that they can be consumed, and value analysis is driven more by supply and demand, including estimates of future supply and demand. (A third investable "supra asset class" is store-of-value assets, which includes things like art and currency.)

Despite all the academic research and interest from the commodity desks of several investment banks, there was little actual money committed to the asset class at the start of the twenty-first century. We estimate that only about $10 billion was tracking commodity indexes by the year 2000. Most of this tended to be institutional, with early adopters including the Harvard endowment, the Ontario Teachers Pension Fund, and two of the largest pension funds in the Netherlands, PGGM and ABP. The Government Investment Company of Singapore also made commodity index investments in the late 1990s.

THE TWENTY-FIRST CENTURY

In the first decade of the twenty-first century, there was a surge in the demand for commodity index investment, accompanied by innovations in the way that the investment was offered. This was no doubt partly due to the pain that equity investors suffered in 2000, making them eager to find another area for investment. While not always successful, commodity investments that tracked indexes generally had shown themselves to be a mechanism for portfolio diversification and inflation hedging. It was also partly due to the fact that the asset class was slowly becoming better understood and that both individuals and institutions had several credible forms of investing available to them. In particular, PIMCO, which was so far known for its fixed-income expertise, began appreciating the benefits of investing in commodity indexes. That firm started managing institutional mandates benchmarked to commodity indexes in 2000. In 2002 it launched a commodity index mutual fund with the innovation that it used U.S. Treasury Inflation Protection Securities (TIPS) as the collateral for commodity exposure, rather than T-bills.

This growth in adoption of index investment products occurred at the same time that supply and demand factors were driving commodity prices higher in many markets. These markets that saw rising prices included wheat, copper, crude oil, and other commodities that were part of published indexes, but also included commodities like rice and steel, which were not part of the mainstream investable indexes. This created a feedback loop where the satisfaction of some of the early adopters was an influence on newer investors. The multiple reasons for investing in commodity indexes led to an estimated $300 billion committed to the asset class by the summer of 2008 (*source:* Barclays Capital). This estimated $300 billion was not only in mutual funds, but also in institutional separate accounts and in exchange-traded funds (ETFs), some of which tracked individual commodities or sectors, rather than having broad-based exposure, and some of which owned physical commodities. Rapidly rising commodity prices during this period could largely be attributed to supply disruptions due to adverse weather and geopolitics, combined with growing demand from the "emerging economies." Nevertheless the investors in commodity indexes, who were generally long-term investors attempting to hedge their inflation exposure as well as their financial risks, were blamed by some for driving up the prices of physical commodities and were even labeled by the oxymoron of "index speculator."

Not surprisingly, the growth in investment tracking indexes led to a proliferation of new indexes being offered to investors. Most of these sprang from the commodity desks of investment banks. Some were kept as proprietary, and some were offered on a transparent basis. This new set of indexes is often referred to as "second

generation," compared with the first generation represented by the
S&P GSCI and DJUBSCI. These second-generation indexes may
simply be designed differently from the first generation in terms of
how and when they roll their futures exposure from a near contract
to a more distant one and where on the futures curve they hold their
exposure; or they may actually be more dynamic and algorithmic.
But to be an index, they should still have a completely specified
means of calculation.

Exhibit 1-2 is a partial list of some of the better-known indexes in
the market that are available from more than one source. Exhibit 1-3
lists some additional proprietary indexes and index families. This could
not be an exhaustive list since new indexes and variations of indexes
are constantly being developed. Furthermore, to list each variation
of an index would be daunting. So in some cases we identify a family
of indexes. Finally, to be included in the primary list (Exhibit 1-2),
we wanted to highlight indexes that are available from more than one
source.

There are also some strategies now offered in the market that
call themselves "indexes" but in fact might better be considered
trading methods. Those strategies indeed follow predefined rules
so that their calculation is transparent, but they could also include
returns that reflect both long and short positions in futures markets. A strategy such as those may indeed have merit, but it may lose
the inherent benefits of diversification and inflation hedging that
the asset class is designed to provide. The back test of a model of
such a strategy may indeed show some potential for diversification
from stocks and bonds as well as some inflation protection, along
with positive returns. But if there is not a fundamental economic
reason to explain those returns, then future inflation protection
and diversification may be of more concern. As such, a long-short
commodity strategy might better be considered more like a hedge
fund—seeking absolute return while happening to invest with the
commodity toolbox. To be considered a measure of the asset class of
commodity investment, an index should incorporate some version
of the characteristics of that first index created in the 1970s, which

Tradable and Transparent Commodity Indexes
- Available from more than one source
- Long-only
- Only commodity futures; no financials

Index	Sponsor	Description	Comments
Dow Jones UBS Commodity Index	Dow Jones and UBS	20 commodities; all sectors	Formerly DJAIGCI; basis for a family of 276 unique indexes, with many more variations posted on ftp site
S&P GSCI	Standard & Poor's	24 commodities; all sectors	Formerly GSCI; basis for a family of indexes
Credit Suisse Commodity Benchmark	Credit Suisse	32 commodities; all sectors	Based on technology of DPCI/JPMCFI; basis for a family of indexes
Rogers International Commodity Index	Beeland Interests, Inc.	37 commodities; all sectors	Developed by James Beeland Rogers. Basis as well for a family of sector indexes
Deutsche Bank Liquid Commodity Index	Deutsche Bank	6 commodities representing energy, precious and industrial metals, and grains	Energy rolled monthly; others rolled annually. Also other indexes in this family, some performance-based
Reuters Jeffries CRB Commodity Index	Jeffries Investment Management	19 commodities; all sectors	Current is tenth revision of original CRB Index
JPMorgan Commodity Curve Index (JPMCCI)	J.P. Morgan	34 commodities; all sectors	Invested across the curve based on open interest. Weights can track GSCI, DJUBSCI, or other indexes
JPM Global Asset Rotator (C-IGAR) Index	J.P. Morgan	12 or 24 commodities, depending on version	Momentum-based indexes

Exhibit 1-2 **Better-Known Indexes, Multiple Providers**

Source: Various index providers

14

Index	Sponsor	Description	Comments
	Deutsche Bank	Variety of performance-based indexes; more variations being added	
Merrill Lynch Commodity Index eXtra	BofA Merrill Lynch	About 450 indexes using 30 commodities with different betas. Alpha indexes based on curve, momentum, volatility, and fundamentals	
	Credit Suisse	Indexes based on fundamental as well as technical factors, one of which includes relative value judgments of Glencore	
	Goldman Sachs	Some proprietary indexes in conjunction with S&P. Also offer index overlay that incorporates relative value judgments of Clive Capital	
	Barclays Capital	"CORALS" index incorporates both fundamental and technical factors	
Greenhaven Continuous Commodity Index	Offered as ETF	Equally weighted. Each month chooses 14 out of universe of 27 commodities based on shape of forward curve	
Summerhaven Dynamic Commodity Index	Offered as ETF	Combines basis and momentum factors. Based on research by Gorton and Rouwenhorst	
JPM Contag	J.P. Morgan	24 commodities in "full energy" version; dynamically selects a point on the futures curve	
Pure Beta Commodity Index	Barclays Capital	18 commodities; all sectors	Seeks a part of the forward curve that is closest to tracking the spot price
Constant Maturity Commodity Index	UBS	27 commodities; all sectors	Holds over multiple maturities depending on shape of forward curve
Backwardated Basket	Morgan Stanley	Usually 9 commodities, all sectors	For each sector of S&P GSCI or DJUBSCI, only most backwardated commodities selected.

Exhibit 1-3 Better-Known Indexes, Proprietary

Source: Various index providers

are also included in the commercially available first- and second-generation indexes. As a reminder, one of these indexes

- Reflects the result of holding long positions and rolling them forward
- Assumes all futures positions are fully collateralized
- Assumes that weighting in some fashion typically reflects relative economic importance of components
- Follows a transparent and fully specified method of calculation

All these indexes and variations, with their fully defined calculations and algorithms, have another common characteristic. They are primarily static, which makes them more useful as an index across different time periods and for historical comparisons and analysis. They do not incorporate a dynamic response to many of the market conditions that ebb and flow in both futures and cash markets. Therefore, while they may be good measures of the asset class of investable commodities, returns can potentially be improved if an investor intelligently replicates one of these indexes, rather than simply following all the transparent rules.

Investment in commodity index strategies has increased tremendously over the last decade, and indexes have become more sophisticated as these markets have become better understood. In our opinion, the goal of investors should not be to just replicate the returns of the asset class as measured by one of these indexes. The goal should and can be to look forward to the next one or two decades and seek to determine how to intelligently position their investments in order to capitalize on the potential benefits offered by this asset class, rather than just relying on back-tested strategies. The goal should be to pick an index that best represents the return potential offered by the asset class and then to attempt to outperform it. We call that "intelligent commodity indexing." Ways to implement that intelligent commodity indexing are described in this book.

CHAPTER 2

Drivers of Commodity Index Returns

The late 1990s were a time when the idea of investing to track a commodity index was becoming better understood, but also a time when few participants were yet to be participating in that form of investment. In fact, at investor conferences, the idea of commodity investing was typically given only one panel position on the conference agenda, while other forms of "alternative" investments, such as hedge funds and real estate, filled out the balance of the program. At one of these events, during the allotted commodity presentation, an advocate of the asset class was heard to say, "Buy oats. There's a shortage of oats. The price is going up." The investor was not, of course, talking about physically owning oats, with the incumbent storage and carrying costs. He was talking about buying oat futures contracts, with the unspoken assumption that those contracts would be fully collateralized. Unfortunately the speaker did not point out that the price of oats for immediate delivery was $2.00 per bushel, whereas the contract for delivery six months later was priced at $2.20. Apparently the market agreed with the speaker—the price of oats was expected to rise. But for that speaker to have made money, the actual price of oats would have had to go up by more than 10% in the next six months.

This story points out a key consideration in commodity investment. With the exception of precious metals, most investors do not buy and own physical commodities. They typically buy fully collateralized commodity futures contracts. They will then roll these futures positions from nearby into distant contracts before the nearby contracts reach the delivery month. As stated earlier, a commodity index measures the return from this form of investment. Index-oriented investors (sometimes simply called *indexers*) also will follow an algorithm to determine relative commodity weights in their portfolio. Typically, the more important the commodity is in world trade, the more important it is in the index.*

The return of a commodity index is thus not driven directly by changes in spot commodity prices but by changes in commodity futures prices (plus a return on collateral). Changes in spot prices will almost certainly impact a change in the price of a futures contract, but the index return will be directly calculated from the futures price, not the spot price. However, at any time, the futures price incorporates the collective expectations of "the market" regarding the future state of the world, along with certain risk premiums that buyers or sellers of these futures demand. So changes in futures prices are caused by "surprises," by changes in expectations of spot prices at a future date, and also by the risk premiums that are inherent in commodity futures contracts. The surprises (e.g., a drought in Russia, an uprising in the Middle East, a strike in a Chilean copper mine) are important because they often cause commodity index returns to be uncorrelated with stocks and bonds, especially if the surprises affect supply expectations. The bond market does not care about short-term disruptions in Chilean copper production, while the commodity markets care deeply about this. The stock market generally does not care about the weather in Russia, which could (and has) meaningfully impacted wheat prices.

---

* For the first description of such an investable commodity index, see Greer (1978). All the major commodity index benchmarks incorporate the same principles established in that work.

But there is even more to the story of how commodity index returns behave. If the investor marketplace decides that inflation will accelerate, bond yields are likely to go up, which hurts bond total returns. Stocks may also be hurt if the market decides that inflation will be higher. But the commodity index is exposed to expected *future prices*. If the world decides that higher inflation is likely, then the expected future prices of some commodities (i.e., commodity futures contracts) may go up. Hence, an investor could have, depending on the type of surprise, something potentially better than lack of correlation with stocks and bonds—namely, negative correlation. This diversification aspect of the commodities asset class is discussed in more detail in Chapter 3.

History has shown that, in fact, commodity indexes are often negatively correlated with equity and fixed-income index returns, but positively correlated with inflation and with changes in inflation over long time horizons. This is partly because of the nature of commodities as a distinct asset class, which means that the drivers of returns to commodity investing tend to be different from other supra asset classes. It is important to understand those drivers of return in order properly to anticipate how commodity investment might fit in a portfolio and also to understand why commodities have performed as they have in various economic events. There is an important question that needs to be answered: if commodity futures markets are efficient, do commodity indexes have an inherent positive real (i.e., inflation-adjusted) return? The answer is yes, and that inherent return does not depend directly on rising commodity prices. The prices of commodity futures contracts already incorporate the collective views on the future state of supply and demand as expressed by the investors, speculators, and trading companies that spend all day, every day, trading in, for example, oat contracts. They use all the information they gain from agricultural analysis and from having representatives in the oat fields of the United States and elsewhere.

The collective market impact, however, also recognizes certain risk premiums that are inherent in the futures markets and that can affect commodity index returns—not only of oats futures but also of other exchange-traded commodities. The commodity index–oriented investor may earn a potential return from several sources, not including a return from a rise in commodity prices that is already expected by the market.

DRIVERS OF COMMODITY INDEX RETURNS

This chapter describes premiums that can accrue to a commodity index from four sources: collateral return, normal backwardation, rebalancing, and something called convenience yield.

Collateral Return

First, the investor may earn a return on the collateral that supports the commodity futures contract. That collateral, for most published indexes, is assumed to be U.S. T-bills. That is because the designers of these indexes did not want their asset class returns made ambiguous by the introduction of risk (either credit risk or interest rate risk) in the collateral. So they chose what has historically been thought of as the "risk-free" asset, T-bills. Over long periods of time, when governments are not actively involved in suppressing short-term interest rates, T-bills have been shown to provide expected inflation plus a small real rate of return. But as we have seen in the extended period of time following the financial crisis of 2008, T-bills can be thought of as, not just the "risk-free" asset, but also the virtually "return-free" asset. Fed actions, including quantitative easing, kept T-bill rates at close to zero for a long period of time. Similarly, interest rate limits after World War II resulted in negative realized real rates on U.S. Treasuries. That is why intelligent indexers, as discussed later in this book, might use some collateral other than T-bills. But whatever that collateral is, it will embody the market's collective expectation of what future inflation will be. That is the nature of capital asset pricing. Here, then, is an important feature of commodity index investing. The investor gets expected inflation, not from the commodities exposure, but from the collateral used. This feature has implications for how to think about using commodities for inflation hedging, a topic discussed in Chapter 3.

Normal Backwardation

The second source of potential return to a long-only commodity investment was identified by John Maynard Keynes long before investable commodity indexes existed. Producers will often pay what can be thought of as an "insurance premium" to ensure a price for future sale of their product. That is, they will sell their product for future delivery at a price lower than where they think the price will actually be in the future. In this way, they stay in business and pass their price risk on to speculators, consumers, processors ... or to long-only investors. The buyer of that contract is paying a price less than where the market thinks the final cash price will really settle. This difference is the insurance premium the buyer earns for assuming the price risk of the producer. Keynes (1930) called that return *normal backwardation*.

Note that the insurance premium is not a function of whether the spot price goes up or down, nor is it a function of whether the forward curve slopes up or down. The term *backwardation* is often used to describe a futures curve that slopes downward. For clarity, that is sometimes referred to as *trader's backwardation*. But normal backwardation is a function of the observed futures price versus the (unobserved) expected future spot price. Keynes's normal backwardation occurs when the futures contract price is lower than where the market thinks the future spot price will be. Although normal backwardation may not exist in all markets (e.g., natural gas, as explained later in this chapter), it apparently exists in most markets, because producers typically have higher inventory and higher fixed costs than buyers of the commodities, who are typically processors or final consumers.

The processors' business model is often that it will pay the market price, add the processor margin, and move the finished product out the door. So processors have less price risk than producers. In fact, if the processors cannot lock in the price at which their finished product will be sold, they might actually be increasing their business risk if they lock in, via a futures contract, the price of one of their inputs.

And what about the final consumers of a commodity? The price of that commodity is only one part, and often a small part, of the total cost structure for the consumers. Since the producers have more concentrated risk in the commodity price than consumers, the producers have greater incentive to hedge their price risk. For example, few consumers would try to hedge their gasoline purchases at the pump by buying gasoline futures. They would not hedge their steak and hamburger consumption by buying live cattle futures. And because the cost of coffee beans represents only a small part of the cost of coffee at a coffee shop, that shop does not have a large economic need to hedge its purchases of its raw material.

This normal backwardation is only part of the story of drivers of commodity index returns. That is fortunate for index-oriented investors, because a reasonable expectation is that as more and more indexers have entered the market providing this insurance to producers, the (unobservable) cost of insurance might go down. That is, commodity index investing is now providing a way for individual consumers to hedge their gasoline purchases or steak consumption, while also potentially providing more efficiently priced hedging to the oil producers and farmers who produce these commodities.

Rebalancing

The next component of return to a commodity index derives from the fact that changes in individual commodity prices are often not highly correlated with one another because they are driven by differing physical and economic events. This lack of correlation is especially true for the supply factor that is part of the supply-demand balance that determines price. The wheat market generally does not care if a strike occurs in Chilean copper mines, and the copper market generally does not care if a freeze affects Brazilian coffee production. As has been shown in some periods, a change in the demand for a commodity, however, might affect several commodities, causing them to have higher correlations with one another. This could especially be true if that change in expected demand results from a change in the outlook for global growth, as will be discussed in Chapter 3. To the extent that individual assets (commodity contracts) are not correlated, then an investor may capture incremental return potential by rebalancing the portfolio: selling what goes up; buying what goes down. This idea of rebalancing was implicit in the pioneering work of Harry Markowitz regarding modern portfolio theory. In his groundbreaking book, *Portfolio Selection*, he wrote:

The Set of Legitimate Portfolios

In the three-security analysis ... we shall let

X_1 represent the *fraction* of the portfolio invested in a first security;

X_2 represent the *fraction* of the portfolio invested in a second security;

X_3 represent the *fraction* of the portfolio invested in a third security.

(Italics added for emphasis)

In a portfolio, once a percentage is assigned to each asset, then to maintain that percentage, some rebalancing is required as prices change. Because individual commodity futures prices tend to be volatile, but often with low correlations with one another, this potential rebalancing component of returns can be attractive. There are varying estimates of the potential benefit of rebalancing. As might be expected, the benefit shown in studies has depended on the frequency of rebalancing, the weighting of the commodities in the index, and the time period over which the study was conducted. If markets are strongly trending, then frequent rebalancing could hurt returns. Ideally the investor would not want to rebalance until the trend began to reverse. On the other hand, if several markets are choppy but still uncorrelated, then more frequent rebalancing would likely be worthwhile.

An early study by Adam De Chiara and Dan Raab (2002) examined returns of the DJAIGCI (now the DJUBSCI) from 1992 to 2002. This index rebalances annually. The authors calculated what the returns would have been if the index had never rebalanced and found that annually rebalancing the index would have provided returns that were higher by an average of 280 basis points (bps) per year.

Bob Greer (2000) calculated rebalancing returns in a different manner. He used the returns of an index that rebalanced daily and that changed weights annually; this is the index described in Chapter 1 as the JPMorgan Commodity Futures Index. To estimate the rebalancing component of the total index returns, he used a formula developed by Fernholz and Shay (1982) and applied it to data from 1970 to 1999. He found that the return from daily rebalancing averaged 248 bps per year and generally increased as the number of commodities in the index increased and as the average cross-correlation decreased.

In a paper published in 2006, Gary Gorton and Geert Rouwenhorst calculated how returns might differ on the basis of frequency of rebalancing. They showed, for instance, that if the index they created were rebalanced annually instead of monthly, the geometric return would have increased by 120 bps per year. This study showed that return can be affected by rebalancing, but it did not develop an explicit attribution to rebalancing return. Further, the optimal frequency of rebalancing should depend on how strongly individual assets are trending during any subperiod.

Credit Suisse performed an analysis of its CSCB, analyzing the returns depending on whether rebalancing was done daily, monthly, quarterly, or semiannually, compared with no rebalancing at all. It used annual time periods from 1998 to 2010. The study found that in only 4 of those 13 years would returns have been greater if the index had not done interim rebalancing.

Unlike Gorton and Rouwenhorst, Erb and Harvey (2006) attributed the entire return of a commodity index (excluding collateral) to rebalancing. This was in a paper published at the same time as

Gorton and Rouwenhorst's work. Erb and Harvey called this rebalancing return "diversification return." It comes not only from selling high and buying low but also, at the portfolio level, from reduced portfolio volatility. Although rebalancing was no doubt a component of their return, their theory cannot explain that during the period of 1982–2004, the GSCI (now the S&P GSCI) had a return that was 4.49% per year above the collateral return. And yet the S&P GSCI never rebalances on the basis of changing prices. It merely reconstitutes once a year on the basis of changes in the quantity of global production. So there must be more to the story than rebalancing, just as there is more to the story than normal backwardation.

Convenience Yield

The next component of return is derived from the fact that, sometimes in some markets, low inventories create a downward-sloping forward curve, referred to earlier in this chapter as trader's backwardation to distinguish it from Keynes's normal backwardation. (By contrast, an upward-sloping forward curve represents "contango.") The shape of the curve is influenced by buyers (processors) paying up for the certainty of supply because they cannot afford to be without their raw materials for even a day. They either bid up the spot price in an attempt to build inventory or bid up the price of the nearby futures contract to ensure that they will be able to obtain inventory (either by taking delivery or by having enough futures profit to pay for the physical commodity regardless of how the price may have moved upward). These processors could, if necessary, take delivery on that contract, but more likely, they will close out that contract at the same time they pay the going market price to their local supplier. The shape and direction of the forward curve can further be influenced by sellers who, in a rising market, may lock in profits by selling forward.

In that environment of a downward-sloping forward curve, the long-only commodity investor naturally is able to sell a high-priced nearby contract and roll into a low-priced distant contract.

If spot prices remain the same, then this distant contract will increase in value as it converges to that spot price, which results in a profit to the indexer. Economists describe this potential return to the long-only investor as a "convenience yield" paid by the buyer of the commodity who wants the *convenience* of a certain supply. This downward-sloping forward curve also indicates that a holder of inventory is better off selling the inventory today at a higher price than in the future at a lower price, thus drawing commodities out of storage to supply the market during times of shortage. This downward-sloping forward curve is often described as creating positive "roll yield," which will be discussed in Chapters 5 and 6.

The description of convenience yield existed long before any investable commodity indexes were created. Kaldor (1939) was an early user of the term from the viewpoint of the commodity buyer. Soon afterward, Working (1949) expanded on the theory of convenience yield as he explained it from the viewpoint of the producer holding inventory and releasing that inventory to the market. This convenience yield is driven primarily by inventory levels, but it can benefit investors if it creates a downward-sloping forward curve that allows them to roll from a high-priced nearby into a low-priced distant contract.

In 2006, an upward-sloping forward curve (contango) arose in crude oil as a result of high crude inventories. Incorrectly, this forward pattern was blamed on "indexers," who would be selling the nearby and buying the distant contract. In 2007, however, about the same amount of index investment occurred, but the crude curve became downward sloping (backwardation) as inventories declined. The point is that the shape of the forward curve tends to be driven much more by the level of crude inventories than by the index participants in the market. Exhibit 2-1 shows graphically the historical relationship between the slope of the crude oil forward curve and the level of inventories. This relationship is consistent with economic theory that existed before investable commodity indexes ever came into existence.

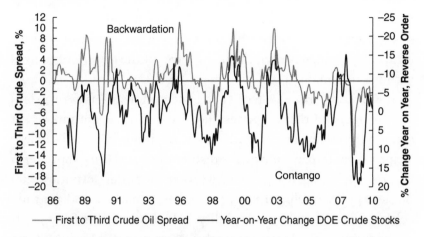

Exhibit 2-1 Basis Chart: Crude Oil Spreads Versus Year-on-Year Change in U.S. Department of Energy Crude Oil Inventory

Source: Bloomberg, as of September 2011

NOT A RISK PREMIUM: EXPECTATIONAL VARIANCE (THAT IS, PRICE CHANGES)

So far, this chapter has explained various sources of potential return to commodity indexes. But another important determinant of returns is surprises, or changes in expectations. These changes in expectations can have a direct impact on the futures contracts of an investable index. As mentioned earlier, the possibility of surprises that change the market's expectations can be the primary driver of the potential diversification benefit of commodity indexes, when the surprise occurs. It is also an important feature that helps explain the inflation hedging qualities of an index-oriented investment, especially in the short run. Over a short period of time—a day, a month, or sometimes even a year—the variance from expectations or price reaction to new information (*expectational variance*, a term coined by Grant Gardner of the Frank Russell Company in the late 1990s) is often the primary driver of commodity index returns. Thus, it may lead to diversification and inflation hedging, as we have explained. But over an extended period of time, an investor must assume that the market will guess too high as often as it will guess too low, so expectational variance is generally not a net source of positive return. It can be, however, the main driver of the pattern of returns within a commodity portfolio.*

Furthermore, the fact that expectations of future prices can change, and that surprises may occur, can benefit intelligent commodity index–oriented investors. As discussed in subsequent chapters, there can be pricing distortions caused by short-term factors, including fear, greed, weather, hedging activities, etc. Because indexers typically have a long-term outlook and are fully collateralized, they have the ability to look at markets from a different perspective than most market participants. This long-term view combined with financial staying power can sometimes give the indexers a cyclical or secular insight on price levels that can be successfully realized over a longer holding period than that of the typical market participant. Put another way, the intelligent indexer does not have to "outguess" the market on directional price moves to add value to a portfolio. And the intelligent indexer can also potentially add value by taking advantage of structural aspects of the markets, including knowledge of market structure, risk premiums, and flow pressures.

THE ECONOMIC FRAMEWORK FOR RETURNS

All these factors suggest that commodity index returns are not driven so much by expected changes in spot commodity prices but by changes in expectations of factors that may affect the future price, as well as by inherent risk premiums, together with a core return on collateral. In summary, long-term published commodity index returns tend to be driven by:

---

* As pointed out by Hilary Till in an unpublished note, however, the noncorrelation of asset class returns introduced to the macro portfolio can be a source of return because it potentially reduces volatility and creates rebalancing of commodities versus stocks and bonds.

- Expected inflation plus or minus a real rate of return from T-bill collateral
- A classical premium for assuming price risk that producers do not want (Keynesian normal backwardation)
- Rebalancing return
- Sometimes, in some markets, a convenience yield

These returns often occur in a fashion that provides a lack of correlation with stocks and bonds (capital assets) and a positive correlation with inflation. It is this expectational variance that often is the primary driver of returns in the short term. Historically, commodity index returns have generally been above that of the underlying collateral. (See Exhibit 2-2 for a sampling of the performance of various indexes over various time periods.) And because commodity futures prices tend to respond to changing microeconomic factors that may not affect stocks and bonds, the returns may often be uncorrelated with equity and fixed-income returns. This is especially true when price changes are affected by supply, rather than demand, expectations. Better yet, to the extent that significant changes in inflation expectations occur, commodity indexes may have a negative correlation with stocks and bonds.

Unfortunately, these economic drivers of return, other than collateral return, do not lend themselves to easy mathematical attribution. The rebalancing return depends on how frequently an index rebalances and on whether one uses the Fernholz and Shay (1982) formula or, instead, simply looks at the returns ex post with and without rebalancing. In addition, if rebalancing is done at a time when weights are changing (because of index rules or the addition of new components), then the rebalancing attribution is affected by the changing index composition. Furthermore, both the Keynesian risk premium and convenience yield are affected by the expectations of market participants regarding what the spot price will be in the future. But we do not see those expectations; we see only the prices at which transactions take place. For the reasons we described, this observed futures price is not the measure of true

Annualized Excess Returns Since Inception

Index	DJUBSCI	S&P GSCI	Gorton & Rouwenhorst Index	CSCB	RICI	DBLCI
Return	1.93%	3.70%	5.11%	6.67%	7.73%	6.25%
Inception Date	January 1991	January 1970	July 1959–December 2007	January 1998	July 1998	January 1988

Exhibit 2-2 Annualized Returns in Excess of Collateral Since Inception Through December 31, 2011

Source: Bloomberg, Gorton & Rouwenhorst

market expectations. This lack of precise quantification, though, does not negate the benefit of understanding fundamental economic relationships. And it is a step forward from the precise quantification of factors that do not reflect fundamental economic relationships.

The economic framework presented here is in contrast to the arithmetic attribution approach that has historically been used. Since many of the factors discussed are in fact unobservable, it makes sense to try to develop a simple yet intuitive framework that can account for the observed returns of a commodity index. This quest led to an arithmetic deconstruction of observed returns into:

- Collateral return
- Spot return
- Roll yield

This arithmetic approach, developed at the same time as the first commercially available index (the GSCI), was a great first step toward understanding the arithmetic (versus economics) underlying the attribution of returns. Roll yield was simply the difference between the nearby contract being sold and the distant contract being bought. If the forward curve sloped down, roll yield was positive. Spot return was the change in the price of the delivery month (spot contract) in that same time period (from the time of a roll to the time of the next roll). If the spot price declined over time to that futures price, then spot return was negative. By definition, total return would equal collateral return plus spot return plus roll yield. If the futures curve precisely predicted where the future spot price would be, then roll yield would be exactly offset by spot return.

As we know, this offset has not frequently happened. The observed spot price (not inflation adjusted) over time for most commodities has gone up since 1970. But the arithmetic model does not reveal how much of this price rise was unexpected. Also, sometimes a forward curve has been downward sloping, and the arithmetic model does not reveal whether that backwardation is caused by convenience yield or whether it simply reflects the expectation that spot prices will be lower in the future. Finally, the arithmetic model doesn't give consideration to returns from rebalancing. While this first-generation attribution model provides the comfort of precise arithmetic, it can be better utilized when combined with the understanding of underlying economics described here. Roll yield (observed) can better be understood if it is thought of as combining aspects of (unobserved) normal backwardation plus convenience yield. Expectational variance (unobserved) provides insight into (observed) spot returns.

NOT ALL COMMODITIES EXHIBIT NORMAL BACKWARDATION

Had an investor held only natural gas futures and rolled them forward each month from January 1994 to December 2009, this hypothetical investor's return would have been a cumulative loss of more than 90% (excluding any collateral return)—in spite of the fact that spot natural gas prices rose by a cumulative 118% in that same period. Where was the Keynesian normal backwardation or any convenience yield? Natural gas represents an unusual situation of negative normal backwardation, which can be exploited by the intelligent commodity indexer.

Unlike the situation for most commodities, the buyers of natural gas have a greater need for risk reduction at the front of the forward curve than do the producers. A utility cannot afford to be without energy supply for a single day; yet it cannot store large quantities of natural gas on-site. The utility might, therefore, pay a higher price than the expected future spot price to ensure that, regardless of immediate supply-demand balances, it can always pay the price to buy gas. (Note that this negative backwardation is different from convenience yield, which tends to occur when industry inventories are actually low.) An investor rolling the nearby natural gas contract monthly is forced to pay this same premium as the power company 12 times a year. Hence, the negative return. Supporting this view is the hypothetical observation that if an indexer for the period 1994–2009 had rolled contracts 12 months ahead—from January to January—the return in excess of T-bills would have been a cumulative positive 14%, much better than the return from rolling monthly. The investor would have been positioned in a distant contract where buyer hedging was not so prevalent, while paying whatever risk premium existed in that distant contract only once a year instead of monthly. This description explains what previously has been a conundrum in commodity investment circles regarding natural gas, and it is discussed in Chapter 7, "Calendar Spreads and Seasonal Strategies."

CONCLUSION

In the early 1990s, arithmetic attribution of returns did the fledgling commodity index industry a great service by showing how analysts could quantify components of index returns. But that arithmetic approach has overshadowed the equally important economics of returns. Recent research has analyzed aspects of those return economics. Once investors understand those economics, they can see that commodity index returns are usually not driven by increases in spot prices if those increases are expected. Rather, returns to the asset class tend to be driven by returns on collateral, enhanced by risk premiums that existed before investable commodity indexes were developed, and enhanced further by the noncorrelation between the prices of specific commodities. Meanwhile, the pattern of returns over shorter time periods will often be determined by changes in market expectations. With this understanding, an investor can better interpret the behavior of commodity index returns and also assess whether or when the historical pattern and magnitude of returns are likely to persist. This framework not only helps the investor understand commodity index behavior but also helps the investor more intelligently to get exposure to the asset class.

As discussed in this chapter, roll yield (a combination of normal backwardation and convenience yield) is a major driver of long-term commodity index returns, while expectational variance or spot price changes generally have the bigger impact in the short term.

Correctly understanding the reasons for the shape of commodity futures curves and using this knowledge to enhance the roll yield of a portfolio that is tracking a commodity index are a major focus of intelligent commodity indexing, which is why we devote both Chapters 5 and 6 to studying this in detail.

CHAPTER 3

Thinking About Inflation Hedging and Diversification

There are two major reasons that investors have been attracted to commodities as an asset class. The first is that commodities, measured by the returns of an investable commodity index, have often provided a hedge against inflation as well as responding positively to it. The second is that commodities have often provided positive returns while showing little or even negative correlation with other financial assets like stocks and bonds. However, these potential benefits don't always occur, typically for the reasons discussed in this chapter. It is important for investors to know what to expect from their commodity index–oriented investments so that they can optimize their asset allocation. This chapter provides an explanation of how to think about commodities in relation to inflation and diversification. We will first consider inflation hedging.

HOW ARE COMMODITY INDEXES RELATED TO INFLATION?

Inflation can be the silent scourge of investors. It doesn't have to be virulent, like the inflation experienced globally in the 1970s, where for a period of time the U.S. CPI was increasing at a double-digit rate. Other countries have also sometimes seen that form of extreme infla- tion. It wasn't just the famous hyperinflation of the German Weimar Republic in 1923 or the recently witnessed inflation of over 11,000% in Zimbabwe in 2007. Greece and Taiwan experienced extreme infla- tion in the mid- to late 1940s after World War II and the Chinese Civil War, respectively, while Brazil in 1994 experienced inflation of over 2,000%. But consider that even with modest inflation of, say, 4% per year, a dollar could lose a third of its purchasing power in 10 years. That is a loss of purchasing power that is needed by people saving for retirement, needed by people in retirement, needed by pension plans to pay their committed benefits, and needed by foun- dations and endowments to pay for salaries, operating expenses, and grants. The higher the rate of inflation, the greater the amount of currency ultimately required by an investor. Therefore, intelligent investors are likely to seek to hedge a part of their portfolios against the possible impact of inflation. Furthermore, more aggressive inves- tors might position their portfolios specifically with the goal of ben- efiting from a future increase in inflation. Commodity investments can often help these types of investors who are concerned with the future level of inflation.

First, it would be helpful simply to look at the historical cor- relation of commodity index returns to inflation. But that becomes a bit difficult because correlations are not stable. The correlation might depend on what commodity index is being observed, what the return periods are (monthly, quarterly, annual), and over what time period the statistics are calculated. For instance, in "Facts and Fan- tasies About Commodity Futures," Gorton and Rouwenhorst (2006) calculated the return of their own index of collateralized commod- ity futures, which was equally weighted and rebalanced monthly. That index was reported from 1960 through 2004. They calculated the correlation of their index to inflation (CPI) over monthly inter- vals, quarterly intervals, annual intervals, and five-year intervals. For completeness, they also calculated the correlation of stocks (S&P 500 Total Return Index) to inflation and of bonds (Ibbotson Corporate

Correlation of Assets with Inflation			
	Stocks	Bonds	Commodities
Monthly	−0.15*	−0.12*	0.01
Quarterly	−0.19*	−0.22*	0.14
1-Year	−0.19	−0.32*	0.29*
5-Year	−0.25	−0.22	0.45*

July 1959 to December 2004

Exhibit 3-1 **Correlation of Asset Classes to Inflation, from G&R**

*Indicates that the correlation is significant at the 5% level using Newey-West corrected standard errors.

Source: G&R

Bond Total Return Index) to inflation over these same intervals. Their findings, shown in Table 5 of their paper, are reported in this chapter as Exhibit 3-1. Commodities had a positive correlation to inflation in all four cases, whether they used monthly returns, quarterly returns, annual returns, or five-year returns. The magnitude of that correlation increased as the observation period got longer. This implies that as the fundamental drivers described in Chapter 2 are given time to manifest themselves, the potential for inflation protection can be increased. Meanwhile, in all these measurement periods, the correlation of stocks to inflation was negative. Likewise, the correlation of bonds to inflation was also negative.

It's pretty easy to understand why bonds have had a negative correlation to inflation. If interest rates rise with inflation, then the mark-to-market value of a bond declines. (Note, however, that TIPS can indeed provide a return highly correlated to inflation when held to maturity.) The situation with stocks is more complicated, since at first glance one would think that stocks ultimately represent holdings of real assets, and real assets should track inflation. But there are other factors in operation. First, if rising inflation leads to higher interest rates, then the discount rate used implicitly to value the future flow of dividends or earnings will be higher, theoretically leading to a lower PE multiple. Second, reported earnings reflect depreciation of historical asset costs, but if inflation is higher, then those assets have a higher replacement cost than is reflected by the depreciation rate. This could affect the quality of the earnings reported. Finally, stocks generally cannot effectively respond to inflation if they cannot pass on higher costs to their customers. In a weak economy, this may be true, potentially leading to stagflation. This discussion does not suggest that equities, over a very long period, cannot exceed the rate of inflation. After all, if given enough time, the equity risk premium should have the effect of providing positive returns. But exceeding inflation over a very long period is not the same thing as responding to inflation, and some investors can't wait the long time that it may take for equities to outperform inflation. In their response to inflation, equities often don't keep up, as shown by the data compiled by Gorton and Rouwenhorst.

These results are comforting to see, but an intelligent investor should look beyond just correlation. For instance, consider two hypothetical portfolios:

- Portfolio A holds 100% in the S&P 500.
- Portfolio B holds 10% in the S&P 500 and 90% in cash.

These two portfolios would in fact have a very high correlation to each other. Remember, positive correlation means that when Portfolio A is doing better than its long-term average, Portfolio B is likewise doing better than its own long-term average. And in this case, because the 10% equity holding will drive the performance and volatility in Portfolio B, when B is doing better than its long-term average it is because equities are doing well—which means that Portfolio A is likewise doing better than its long-term average. Even though these two portfolios would have a very high correlation, they would still likely have quite different returns. If stocks double in price, Portfolio A would earn a 100% return, while Portfolio B would earn only a 10% return (plus the return on cash). So Portfolio B has a muted response to equities. It would have a beta of 0.10 to equities.

With this distinction in mind, an investor may seek an inflation hedge that is not just correlated to inflation, but that has a high "inflation beta." Equally important, since it is also changes in inflation, rather than just the level of inflation, that can drive changes in the price of financial assets, an investor needs an asset class that is particularly sensitive to *changes* in inflation—that has a high beta to inflation changes.

Several factors should be considered in relating commodity index returns to inflation, including the following:

- Food and energy (i.e., commodities) tend to be the most volatile component of the headline CPI.*
- Because commodity index returns reflect *changes* in futures prices, they inherently reflect *changes* in the expectation of what actual cash prices in the future will be.
- The return on the collateral that supports a commodity index often incorporates the inflation *expected* at any time by market participants; but as we have seen in 2010–2011, some types of collateral in fact can't keep up with inflation.

With this background, consider that the collateral return of a commodity index, rather than the commodity exposure itself, can incorporate some hedging from *expected* inflation. (The interest rate demanded on the collateral will be high if inflation is expected to be high.) T-bills, depending on the era studied, have generally yielded inflation plus a (small) real return. Because T-bills are classically considered the "risk-free" asset, and because T-bills can be posted as margin in commodity futures accounts, published indexes usually assume that T-bills are used to collateralize the futures contracts that are used to calculate an index.

However, investors have occasionally been reminded that in periods like 2010 and 2011, or like some of the hyperinflationary

---

* Headline CPI is an inflation figure released monthly by the U.S. Bureau of Labor Statistics, which includes "core" inflation plus food and energy inflation.

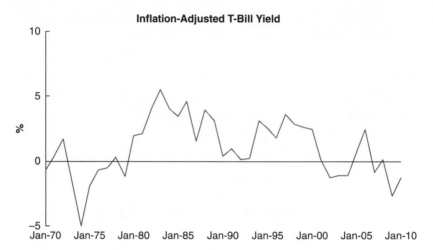

Exhibit 3-2 **Historical T-Bills Returns Adjusted for Inflation**

Source: Bloomberg

years of the 1970s, T-bills cannot just be considered the risk-free asset, but can also be considered the *return-free* asset. Exhibit 3-2 shows a long history of inflation-adjusted T-bill returns. Negative real yields on short-term fixed-income securities can be affected by actions of policy makers, who might have an incentive to keep interest rates below the rate of inflation. Consequently, investors in practice may use another form of collateral, such as enhanced cash or TIPS, in order potentially to enhance their after-inflation yield (a topic discussed in Chapter 10, "Implementation"). But whatever the collateral, like any other asset, it will embed the market's collective expectation at that time of what inflation will be. (Likewise, other financial assets, including stocks, inherently reflect the market's inflation expectations.)

It is, however, *unexpected* inflation, or changes in inflation expectations, that can have an impact on financial assets. For instance, if the markets experienced a surprise increase in inflation or an increase in inflation expectations, then it is likely that bond yields would go up, which would cause bond prices to go down. Depending on other aspects of the economy, stocks prices might also suffer during a period of rising inflation expectations, as already discussed in this chapter. In most cases, unexpected or sudden changes in inflation or inflation expectations are caused by changes in commodity prices, since food and energy tend to be the most volatile component of most measures of inflation. Hence commodity futures exposure can add, over time, a natural response to this unexpected inflation (plus incremental return potential resulting from the risk premiums discussed in Chapter 2).

So $1 invested in a commodity index–oriented investment in most cases can be expected to provide $1 of hedging from expected inflation because of the return on collateral, except when the real yield on that collateral is negative—which is when the intelligent index investor can move to more attractive fixed-income securities. *Unexpected* inflation, which is the greater worry of most investors, will more likely be captured by the futures component of a commodity index. The exception, when the collateral portfolio could also see positive returns in the face of unexpectedly higher inflation, may be when the collateral is invested in TIPS or other inflation-sensitive securities. The percentage change in the price of commodities is often a multiple of the change in headline CPI. Changes in realized inflation, whether expected or unexpected, will be driven in the short to intermediate term more by changes in the most volatile component, food and energy, than by changes in other components, such as housing costs. Food and energy represent, according to the U.S. Bureau of Labor Statistics, about 25% of the U.S. CPI, but have typically been the drivers of over half the total volatility of the CPI.

This effect is even stronger in some emerging economies, in which food and energy are a higher component of CPI than in the United States. Food and energy represent more than 25% of most commodity indexes, and so the directional changes in commodity futures returns should be an exaggeration of the moves in the CPI. This exaggerated effect is even stronger if you consider that only a portion of the food and energy prices in the CPI is the actual cost of the raw material; yet the cost of that raw material is often the main driver of changes in the finished good. As an extreme example, consider that with wheat priced at $7 per bushel, a $3 box of Wheaties might contain less than 15 cents' worth of raw wheat. So if wheat doubled in price, the direct impact on Wheaties (and thus on the CPI) is much less than the 100% increase in wheat prices. Moreover, the collateral component of a commodity index actually reflects the expected changes in food and energy prices, leaving the futures component to capture the unexpected changes. Therefore, one might expect the total return of a commodity index to reflect an exaggerated response to changes in total CPI.

This exaggerated response can be measured by calculating the beta in a simple regression where the *change* in inflation is the independent variable and commodity returns are the dependent variable. (It should not be too much of a stretch to think of the change in inflation to be a surrogate for unexpected inflation—one need only assume that the market believes that future inflation will be the same as current inflation, and research tends to support that assumption.) Exhibit 3-3 shows the calculation of this "inflation beta" for various

	S&P GSCI	**DJUBSCI**	**G&R***
1960–2007	NA	NA	**1.6** (0.08)
1971–2007	**1.1** (0.02)	NA	**1.5** (0.06)
1971–2009	**2.8** (0.11)	NA	NA
1987–2007	**8.7** (0.18)	NA	**4.1** (0.14)
1987–2009	**13.7** (0.50)	NA	NA
1992–2007	**11.7** (0.13)	**7.6** (0.14)	**7.5** (0.23)
1992–2009	**17.0** (0.50)	**10.8** (0.46)	NA

Exhibit 3-3 **Inflation Beta Calculation**

*Numbers in boldface are measured by using CPI-U (the CPI for urban consumers). Numbers in parentheses are R^2s.

Source: Bloomberg, G&R (rolling 12-month calculations). G&R constructed an equally weighted collateralized futures index.

indexes, with the R^2s in parentheses over various periods of time. For instance, in the 1992–2009 period, a 1% *change* in inflation would have been associated with a 10.8% change in the DJUBSCI (along with a lot of noise). Although the results are statistically significant, the R^2s are low, indicating that although inflation can explain a portion of commodity returns, many other factors also affect commodity index returns, as described in Chapter 2. Nevertheless, $1 of collateralized commodity index investment, with the associated noise, might be used to hedge more than $1 of inflation-linked liabilities from changes in inflation. And it is often *changes* in inflation, rather than inflation itself, that can affect the prices of financial assets. Bonds, for instance, might not be hurt by a high level of inflation if it were stable and predictable. Interest rates might also be high but stable. However, as discussed already, bondholders would certainly suffer pain as interest rates moved from a low level to a higher level.

As for the betas, the exhibit shows that inflation betas increased after 1987, when crude oil entered many commodity indexes. This is not surprising. Nor is it surprising that an index that had a large energy component would have a higher inflation beta than an index with a small energy component. After all, energy is a very important component of the cost of living. However, as shown in the hyperinflation of the 1970s, when energy was not in indexes, the overall asset class may still have provided valuable inflation protection qualities. In other words, energy exposure is an important part of inflation hedging, but this inflation hedging is about much more than just energy. When assessing commodity indexes, their expected relative response to inflation is one factor to consider, along with their expected volatility and their expected response to the drivers of return described in Chapter 2.

Finally, another factor that relates inflation to commodity returns is the value of the investor's home currency. If the value of that currency declines, then the cost of imports will increase, driving up the rate of inflation. For instance, if the value of the U.S. dollar declines, then anything priced in U.S. dollars will increase, including the price of real assets like commodities.

HOW TO THINK ABOUT COMMODITIES FOR DIVERSIFICATION

One way of thinking about the diversification features of commodities is that although they are investable assets, they are not
capital assets and therefore are driven by economic factors that are
different from the factors driving capital assets. Capital assets can
be valued using a discounted present value of futures payments,
such as dividends, earnings, or interest payments. But commodities don't generate a stream of payments. Commodities have value
because they can be consumed—or transformed into something
that can be consumed. Again, precious metals, gold in particular,
are an exception to this type of valuation, though gold is still not
a capital asset since it does not generate a stream of payments.
Rather, gold represents a store of value, similar to art or currencies.
So in fact there are three investable "supra asset classes"—capital
assets, consumable assets, and store-of-value assets. Commodities
are generally in the second of these supra asset classes, but with
some characteristics of store-of-value assets if in fact they can be
effectively stored. This can become an additional factor in commodity valuation in a period of skepticism about the endurance
of fiat currencies and debt monetization by central banks. To the
extent that a particular commodity has some store-of-value characteristics, its valuation might be influenced by the level of interest rates and changes in those rates. However, to the extent that
commodities are also (or primarily) consumable assets, we believe
supply-demand analysis is a better way to assess the value than is
net present value analysis (see Greer, 1997).

We have already seen in this book the correlation statistics
that support the case for the potential diversification benefit of commodities. But it is also helpful simply to think of specific situations
where commodities provided helpful diversification. For instance,
as shown in Exhibit 3-4, when Iraq invaded Kuwait in 1990, commodities provided a positive response to offset the negative impact
that this unexpected event had on the stock market (as represented
by the S&P 500).

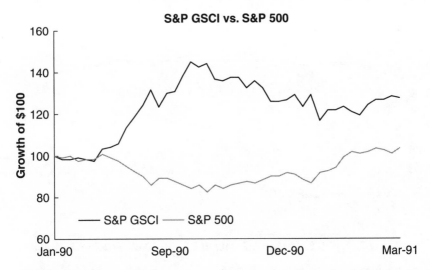

Exhibit 3-4 Performance of Commodity Index and Stocks During the Persian Gulf War

Source: Bloomberg

Another case where commodities provided diversification from adverse stock returns was October 1987. A sudden loss of liquidity seized the equity markets, which went into free fall. But as shown in Exhibit 3-5, commodity indexes were virtually unchanged. The stock market decline did not immediately cause a worldwide recession, with any accompanying decrease in expected demand. People continued to drink their coffee, eat their steaks (or maybe just switched to hamburgers), and drive their cars. There was no serious change in the supply and demand for commodities during this period. This represents the fundamental economic diversification—risk factor diversification—that commodity indexes can often provide.

Commodity prices are usually driven by factors that are very different from those that determine the price returns of traditional asset classes. These include microlevel weather patterns—poor rainfall in the Ukraine affects global wheat prices; a delayed monsoon in India affects global sugar prices; a hotter or colder than expected

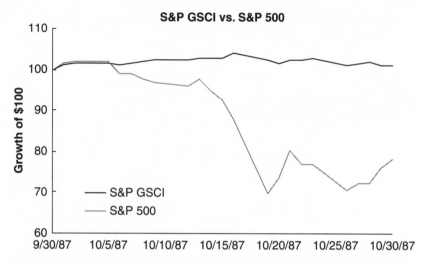

Exhibit 3-5   Performance of Commodity Index and Stocks in October 1987

Source: Bloomberg

year affects U.S. natural gas prices; localized geopolitical risk, such as civil strife in Nigeria, affects global oil prices; unrest in the Ivory Coast affects global cocoa prices; and strikes for better working conditions in Chile can affect global copper prices.

Moreover, just as in the case of inflation hedging discussed earlier, a small amount of capital allocated to a commodity index strategy can go a long way in diversifying or reducing the overall volatility of a portfolio of stocks and bonds. This is simply because the negative correlation and higher volatility of commodities combine with the existing portfolio to have a large dampening effect on the overall portfolio volatility. If an asset has negative correlation to the rest of a portfolio, then its diversification benefit is greater if the asset is more volatile.

This potential for diversification has historically worked often, but not always. After every meltdown of multiple markets, people will ask, "Where is my diversification when I need it?" That question was certainly asked following the global financial crisis in the second half of 2008. It was also asked in the summer of 1998, when the crisis caused by the implosion of Long-Term Capital

Management (LTCM) caused stock markets to decline—without favorable offset from commodity markets. No doubt the question will be asked again in any occasion when commodities generally fail to zig while stocks and bonds zag. The simple answer is that diversification does not guarantee that one asset will go up when another goes down. At the fundamental level, diversification means that the prices of different assets tend to be driven by different risk factors. And so diversification of risk factors within a portfolio should be an investor's important objective when seeking overall risk reduction. The point is that although the fundamental drivers of price returns can be very different, technical drivers can take over at times of market stress and overwhelm the fundamentals.

Consider what happened to commodity indexes in the recession that began in very late 2007. From 2007 through the first half of 2008, the futures (and cash) markets were searching for a price that balanced supply and demand in many commodity markets where supply was constrained in the face of synchronized global growth. These supply constraints included one-off weather-related events such as poor rainfall in Chile that curtailed hydropower generation to copper mines and a crippling snowstorm and earthquake in China that affected coal supplies there. At this time in early 2008, any market participants who recognized an incipient recession thought it was just a U.S. problem that globally could be offset by growth in emerging markets. Both supply and demand for commodities were quite inelastic in the short run. Because of this low short-term elasticity, prices rose, seeking a level that would balance demand and supply. Eventually high prices, combined with the incipient recession, began to have their logical effect—demand dropped. In the face of inelastic supply, it was reasonable that the drop in demand would take a toll on prices. The impact was manifested early in the U.S. gasoline market. According to the Energy Information Administration, in a recession and facing $4 per gallon for gasoline, U.S. drivers drove fewer vehicle miles during the summer of 2008 than in the previous summer, something that had not occurred for over two decades. This reduction in gasoline consumption caused a decline in expectations of future demand, which in turn drove down expectations of future prices. Then came the global liquidity crisis, taking the world from the expectation of a (small r) recession to a (capital R) Recession. Immediately after the bankruptcy of Lehman Brothers, there was a liquidity crisis, as years of leverage built into the financial system during the benign times of the "Great Moderation" had to be unwound quickly. This led to a simultaneous and unco-ordinated attempt by market participants to shed risk of every sort, with credit, equity, and commodity positions all being liquidated. However, in the credit and equity markets, all the liquidation was being attempted by just one side, the long side, since those mar-kets had many sellers and few buyers. At least in commodity futures, where there are as many short as long positions, the liquidity crisis was less severe. But nevertheless global trade ground to a halt as settlement systems were in disarray, recession caused a decline in commodity demand, and commodity prices also severely declined. This was exacerbated by the fact that some commercial interests, needing liquidity, reduced their level of physical inventories.

Exhibit 3-6 shows how stocks, bonds, and commodity indexes fared during the global financial crisis of 2008. Exhibit 3-7 also shows how the various sectors of the commodity markets (energy, agricultural, industrial metals, precious metals, livestock) performed during the crisis in 2008 and during the recovery in 2009. In 2008 all sectors suffered. Gold, which often acts more like a currency than a commodity, suffered the least. But note that in 2009 demand started improving as stimulus and crisis prevention packages put in place by several governments began to work. Supply factors reas-serted themselves, and commodity prices recovered. Moreover, once the synchronous drop and then recovery in all commodity prices completed its course, fundamentals in individual commodity mar-kets started reasserting themselves, leading to more dispersion in the returns of various commodities.

The decline of 2008 was not the first time commodities failed to provide some degree of protection from a free fall in stock prices. From mid–1997 through 1998, commodity index returns were nega-tive because global demand was unexpectedly reduced by the Asian

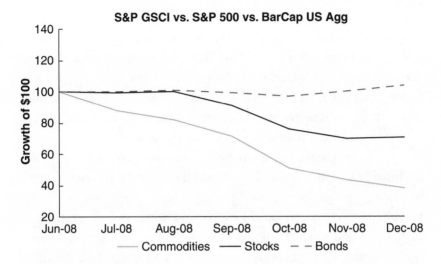

Exhibit 3-6 **Return of Stocks, Bonds, and Commodities in the Second Half of 2008**

Source: Bloomberg

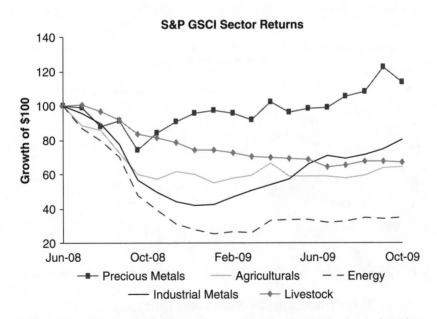

Exhibit 3-7 **Performance of Major Commodity Sectors in the Second Half of 2008 and the First Half of 2009**

Source: Standard & Poor's

currency crisis, followed by the collapse of the ruble and other effects of a surprise global recession. (Meanwhile, OPEC, in an attempt to maintain market share, kept pumping oil in the face of declining demand, which caused a severe decline in energy prices.) During this time, LTCM imploded, causing a severe break in equity prices in the summer of 1998. Where was the diversification benefit of owning commodities when LTCM came along?

Unfortunately, as shown by Exhibit 3-8, commodity prices declined before, during, and after the LTCM crisis. But that decline had nothing to do with LTCM. Rather, the market was adjusting to a change in expectations of supply and demand. Expectations of global demand were changing. Diversification in risk factors does not guarantee diversification of returns. And sometimes a common risk factor, such as the overall level of global growth, will be more dominant than any supply factors, though often the unique risk factors of commodities can help. For instance, consider the returns described by Gorton and Rouwenhorst at times of extreme stock market declines. They identified the months, from 1959 to 2004,

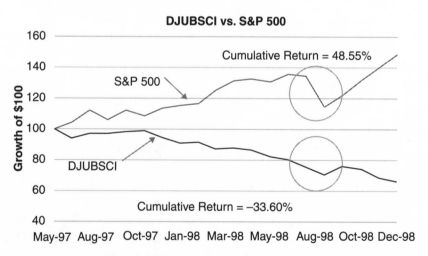

Exhibit 3-8 **Performance of Stocks and Commodities During LTCM's Implosion**

Source: Bloomberg

in which occurred the 5% worst performance by equities. During those really bad months, equities (S&P 500) dropped an average of 8.98% a month, while their commodity index experienced a positive return of 1.03%. They then examined a more extreme sample—the months that contained the worst 1% of stock market performance. In those months, the average stock market return was a negative 13.87%, while their commodity index returns were a positive 2.38%.

The framework established here also highlights the idea that there is more likely to be a diversification benefit when expectational variance occurs in supply (affecting a single commodity) rather than in demand (which can affect a broad swath of commodities as well as financial assets). There are no guarantees in the financial markets, just as there are no predictions that are absolutely correct. But as Markowitz said in *Portfolio Selection*, "Economic forces are not understood well enough for predictions to be beyond doubt or error.... We are expecting too much if we require the security analyst to predict with certainty."

However, those security analysts, and other investors, must still make decisions under uncertainty. The potential for diversification and inflation response that often accompanies commodity index investment may help provide a better expected outcome in a world where they can't be sure of what to expect.

In these last two chapters, we have described the drivers of commodity index returns and explored how this often leads to the benefits of diversification and inflation hedging. This should lay the groundwork for a detailed analysis of intelligent commodity index investing, or how to retain the potential inflation hedging and diversification benefits while exploiting risk premiums and inefficiencies in the market in an attempt to provide superior returns.

CHAPTER 4

Intelligent Commodity Indexation Overview

We have described how various commodity indexes can represent the asset class and how that asset class can, over time, potentially provide benefits of diversification and inflation hedging while offering returns that may be comparable to equities in magnitude and volatility. All those indexes have the common characteristics of representing returns from an investment process that:

- Holds long positions in a variety of futures contracts of actual commodities (i.e., no financial futures)
- Assumes that all positions are fully collateralized, usually by T-bills in the index calculation
- Has a completely described and transparent methodology for determining which contracts will be held, how contracts will be rolled forward, and what the relative weighting of the commodities will be

All these indexes share a common trait—they are all static in the sense that they, by definition, must follow explicit rules for investment. Otherwise, they would not be indexes. No static index can adequately respond to all the changing characteristics of the many individual commodity markets that are represented in the index. These dynamic characteristics can reflect changing risk premiums in either the futures or cash markets. They can also represent uniquely occurring supply and demand factors or pressure from transaction flows in the markets. For instance, risk premiums in agricultural markets may change as weather or crop conditions change. A static index is not "programmed" to respond to these situations.

But a situation might, for instance, affect the shape of the forward curve, which can influence where intelligent investors hold their positions in a specific market. Active investors can take advantage of these factors and potentially generate "structural alpha" over the return of the index, even without making an outright bet on the direction of spot commodity prices, if they study and understand the commodity markets. In doing so, the intelligent index-oriented investors have an advantage over the totally passive market participants, who by definition strictly follow the dictates of the chosen index regardless of its inefficiencies and regardless of changing structural features of the cash and futures markets. Those totally passive investors are essentially "price takers," willing to accept whatever price the market demands, while neglecting these opportunities for structural alpha that naturally occur. Intelligent commodity index investors do not need to take a view on short-term price movements, but may still outperform a commodity index by a combination of careful execution and exploitation of structural liquidity and risk premiums along with clientele effects.

The generation of structural alpha, or excess return over that of the commodity index, without taking explicit views on the direction of individual commodity prices is the essence of what this book is about. We call it *intelligent* commodity indexing, because anything else, by definition, would be ... well, passive! This alpha is generated by exploiting recurring risk and liquidity premiums in the commodity markets. It also involves seeking to avoid inefficiencies in the construction of static commodity indexes and exercising careful execution of trades and futures rolls. Furthermore, often the choice of three-month T-bills as collateral backing the commodity futures is not particularly intelligent, and we discuss how choosing and managing the fixed-income collateral backing the commodity futures can add a further structural alpha component to a commodity index portfolio.

Let us illustrate components of structural alpha generation with examples from the more familiar and well-studied bond and equity markets. Bond market yield curves are usually upward sloping, a shape that allows for a well-functioning financial system that profits from borrowing short and lending long. Given this fact, bond investors may structurally choose to maintain a longer duration (or average maturity) in their portfolio relative to their index or benchmark. As long as the yield curve is upward sloping, this extension can pick up incremental yield or carry relative to the index. Similarly, in equities, one may find that investing in less liquid small-cap stocks in the same industry can lead to higher long-term returns than investing in similar large-cap names (though perhaps with greater risk), since by doing so one avoids paying the "liquidity premium" embedded in the price of the more familiar (and usually more liquid) large-cap name. It is similar strategies, which may underperform in the short term but have the potential to result in long-term outperformance for the patient and disciplined investor, that we discuss in the rest of this book.

Most of the remaining chapters of this book, summarized below, describe the rich opportunity set available to investors who are seeking structural alpha in addition to the beta of their chosen index. These strategies are driven by risk premiums, flow pressures, storage costs, and other structural aspects of the cash and futures markets.

- Chapters 5 and 6 discuss the concept of roll yield, or the return that can be gained or lost by rolling commodity exposure from one futures contract to another. As investors sell a nearby contract and replace it with a more distant contract, they will either be selling high and buying low or vice versa, depending on the shape of the forward curve. Understanding and managing this aspect—the roll yield—is one of the most important elements of long-term commodity investing; hence we devote two chapters to it.

- Chapter 7 discusses strategies based on seasonal variations in commodity prices. Planting and harvest seasons, holiday driving seasons, heating and cooling seasons all have impacts on the demand, either actual or perceived, for specific commodities. Understanding these seasonal effects and how they change risk premiums can help generate excess returns.

- Chapter 8 shows how the same basic exposure to a commodity can often be expressed more efficiently in a market other than the market used to calculate the value of the chosen index. The essentially identical commodities traded in different markets may be subject to different supply and demand fundamentals, hedging activity, speculative attention, differing degrees of liquidity, or different storage costs. Any of these factors could lead to the outperformance of one essentially identical commodity over another traded in a different market.

- Chapter 9 explains how hedging and transaction pressures can create structural opportunities for the buying and selling of volatility in futures markets. The judicious selling of options may be another structural generator of positive returns, as buyers of insurance and lottery tickets generally tend to overpay. In addition, often there are times when option-related deal flow will result in it being cheaper and more effective to replicate a position using options rather than futures or swaps.

- Following descriptions of the structural strategies used by intelligent index-oriented investors, Chapters 10 and 11 describe the very important aspects of how to implement commodity index exposure, including a deep discussion of risk management, which is essential for effective execution. In these chapters, we also discuss how both the choice and management of collateral backing the commodity futures can be a further source of structural alpha.

- Chapter 12 recognizes that commodity prices are indeed affected by the fundamental economics of the individual markets and that an understanding of market fundamentals may help an indexer determine whether to rely on historical patterns of risk premiums. Therefore this chapter describes some of the many sources of fundamental economic information available to an investor.

- Chapter 13 then takes a look at likely new developments in commodity indexes and also describes how an intelligent index investor should view many of these new strategies that will continue to be offered by dealers and investment managers.

CHAPTER 5

The Drivers of Roll Yield

As already discussed in Chapter 2, roll yield is the normalized difference in price between a nearby and a deferred commodities future contract. It is the return that would be earned from rolling a commodity futures contract from one month to the next if there were no change in spot prices. Since long-term commodity index–oriented investors are constantly rolling their futures exposure, it is important to understand the impact this can have on holding period returns. As a matter of fact, it is one of the most important drivers of long-term returns for commodity index investors, and so we devote two chapters of this book to understanding and enhancing the roll yield of a portfolio.

For example, if the price of the front-month oil futures contract is $80 and the price of the next month's oil futures contract is $79.50, then when investors roll their exposure from the nearby to the next month's contract, they lower their cost basis by 50 cents. If the spot price of oil remains unchanged at $80 over that month, then investors will realize a profit of 50 cents as the futures contract converges to the spot price. For a long-term investor, roll yield can be a tailwind that boosts returns, as in the case above, but at other times it can be a headwind that causes returns to lag the returns of the spot commodity. This is why roll yield is of such great concern for commodity index–oriented investors. Over the short run, it is the change in each commodity's spot price that is the dominant driver of daily, weekly, and monthly returns. However, over longer time horizons, roll yield can have both dramatic positive and negative effects.

For example, from the end of 1998 to October 2004, the price of crude oil rose from $12 to over $50, a gain of 330%. However, the gain from rolling front-month futures over that six-year span was 636%. The roll yield in crude oil contributed an extra 306% to returns over that six-year period. This period stands in stark contrast to what happened in 2009 when commodity prices came roaring back after the credit crisis in 2008 subsided. In 2009 oil rose from a low of $34 all the way to $80, a nearly 80% increase. However, rolling front-month futures only returned 7%. When roll yield causes underperformance, it generates significant concern among many investors, and much attention is given to the issue; but it seems to be largely ignored when it produces substantial positive returns.

In this chapter, we will work to separate fact from fiction regarding roll yield by taking a long-term, analytical approach. In order to do this, we will look at how to quantify roll yield by decomposing it into basic, fundamental factors. We will also demonstrate the extreme importance of roll yield in long-term commodity index returns. Finally, we will use our fundamental decomposition of roll yield to look at how an investor can seek to maximize roll yield and thereby maximize long-term return potential.

Roll yield was a concept originally introduced as a tool to help provide attribution of commodity index returns to investors. As explained in Chapter 2, roll yield was defined as the difference between the return realized from an uncollateralized investment in commodity futures (excess return) and the percentage change in the underlying spot price of the commodity (spot return).

$$R_{\text{excess}} = R_{\text{spot}} + R_{\text{roll yield}}$$

Roll yield is essentially the carry of a commodity index investment. If spot prices never moved, then all returns from an uncollateralized index investment that did not rebalance would have to
be attributable to roll yield; hence the roll yield is just the carry.
Suppose investors are rolling out of their currently held contract
and rolling into some deferred contract. In that case, the roll yield
can be expressed as:

$$\text{Roll yield} = \frac{P_{\text{current}} - P_{\text{deferred}}}{P_{\text{current}}}$$

If the price of the deferred contract is above the price of the
current contract, then the roll yield will be negative. For example,
if the price of a front-month crude oil futures contract is $80 and
the deferred contract being rolled into is priced at $80.81, then the
roll yield is −1% for that time period. Put another way, if the investors previously held 100 contracts at a price of $80, after rolling
to the deferred contract at a price of $80.81, the investors would
only hold 99 contracts in order to maintain the same amount of
notional dollar exposure. The investors hold 1% fewer contracts
for the same amount of dollar notional, i.e., a roll yield of −1%.
The investors didn't actually lose money when rolling, but they
did lose exposure. Similarly, if the price of crude oil in the front
month is $80 and the deferred contract being rolled into is priced
at $79.20, then the investors would hold 101 of the deferred con-
tracts to maintain the same dollar exposure. The investors would
hold one additional contract, i.e., a roll yield of +1%. In either case,
if the investors had closed out their position the day after rolling
and prices opened unchanged, then they would not have made or
lost any money. When an investor or an index rolls their exposure
forward, the roll yield return is completely offset by an equal and
opposite spot price return.

Roll yield itself does not generate any profits or losses. What
happens to the futures price after the roll has been completed will

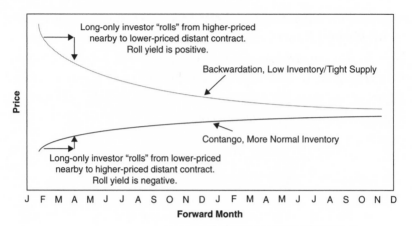

Exhibit 5-1 Examples of Commodity Curves with Positive and Negative Roll Yield

determine whether there is profit or loss. In reality, roll yield just determines the change in the quantity that is owned. From the above example, we see that when the roll yield is negative, investors reduce the quantity owned; and when roll yield is positive, they increase the quantity owned. Therefore, another way to think of roll yield is as an opportunity cost or benefit that investors will realize from continually rolling a long exposure in a given commodity or commodity index.

Examples of a commodity curve with positive and negative roll yield are shown in Exhibit 5-1. When a commodity curve is upward sloping and the price of the deferred contracts is above the price of the nearby contracts—i.e., the roll yield is negative—then the curve is said to be in *contango*. On the other hand, when the price of the deferred contracts is below the price of nearby contracts, then the curve is said to be in *backwardation*. Next we will consider why commodities have these two different curve shapes and what can cause them to switch from one type to the other.

THE RATIONALE

To consider the relationship between the forward and current price of a commodity, it is best to think of it from the perspective of a physical market participant. A physical market participant is involved with the actual physical commodity in some way, such as production, storage, processing, or consumption. Suppose a physical oil trader entered into a transaction where he purchased a nearby futures contract and sold a longer-dated futures contract. Since the nearby futures contract gives the trader the right to take delivery of oil on a certain date, the physical trader could hold the nearby contract into delivery and take delivery of the physical oil. The trader could then store the oil and ultimately deliver it back against the longer-dated contract that he had sold. Excluding transaction costs, the cost that the trader incurs would be the storage cost associated with holding the physical oil plus the financing cost for the funds used to pay for the oil. This cost of storage plus financing is often referred to as *full carry* because it represents the full costs associated with buying and carrying a position in the physical commodity itself. Full carry is the most negative that the spread between two different contracts in the same commodity should trade under normal circumstances, since more negative spreads would allow for physical arbitrage opportunities. However, the spread between contracts could trade at a less negative spread than full-carry if physical participants found some value to holding the physical commodity. This value of holding the physical commodity is often referred to as the *convenience yield*. The convenience yield can be thought of as implied or imputed because it is not a physically observable number; rather it is implied based upon the spread between current futures prices and the full-carry costs. By using the concept of convenience yield, the roll yield can be expressed as:

$$\text{Roll yield} = \text{convenience yield} - \frac{\text{storage cost} + \text{financing cost}}{P_{\text{current}}}$$

Recall that the roll yield is the opportunity cost or benefit for an index-oriented investor in a given commodity. The cost of holding the physical commodity is the storage plus financing costs.

Therefore, the convenience yield represents the relative opportunity cost or benefit of holding a financially based commodity futures position versus a position in the physical commodity itself (part of this is explained by normal backwardation as discussed in Chapter 3 and again later in this chapter). If the convenience yield in a given commodity is positive over the long term, then the roll yield will be better than the cost of full carry. This means that the opportunity cost or roll yield for a long-term buy-and-hold investor will be lower in a commodity index, i.e., rolling futures, than the cost of holding the physical commodity. Similarly, if the convenience yield could be shown to be structurally negative, the long-term investor would be better off holding the physical commodity itself rather than commodity index exposure, as the roll yield would be worse than the cost of full carry.

COPPER, AN EXAMPLE

Using the above principles, let's look at the roll yield of copper in detail. In this example, we will look at the roll yield between the second and third London Metal Exchange (LME) copper contract. First, we calculate the spread between the price of the second and third LME copper contracts (P2–P3). This price spread is converted to a yield by dividing by the price of the second LME copper contract. The advantage of using the roll yield over the price spread is that the roll yield is normalized by the price of the underlying commodity, which makes comparisons across different time periods and different price regimes more meaningful. The line in Exhibit 5-2 shows the historic roll yield between the second and third LME copper contracts. The roll yield between these copper contracts has averaged 1.4% for the past 12 years. This 1.4% roll yield means that an investor just buying and rolling a long copper position would have earned an additional 1.4% per year above and beyond any spot price returns. The 1.4% represents the yield or the opportunity benefit that has accrued to the investor owning

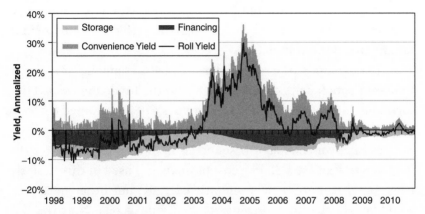

Exhibit 5-2   Roll Yield of Copper Decomposed

Source: Bloomberg, PIMCO, LME, as of June 30, 2011

and rolling copper futures over the past 12 years. Note that this is in excess of the storage and financing cost of holding physical copper. Traders ascribe a high convenience yield to holding physical copper; hence owning copper synthetically in futures is actually cheaper and more efficient than owning the physical commodity.

The exhibit also shows how roll yield tends to move in fairly long trends. For the first five years from 1998 to 2003, the roll yield was negative; then for the next five years, it was positive; and for the final two years, it hovered around zero. The point of this is that it is important not to naively extrapolate the future roll yield of a commodity from just historical roll yields. A commodity's roll yield is a reflection of physical, fundamental factors that evolve over time. While much has been made about the negative roll yield of the DJUBSCI and the S&P GSCI over the past five years, the chart of the copper roll yield shows the potential problem with extrapolating solely from these past results. Merely citing that the roll yield for a certain commodity or index has been negative for the prior five years is not justification to claim it will be negative for the next five. Therefore, in order to make a fair assessment of the future roll yield for individual commodities and commodity indexes, it is necessary to understand the different fundamental factors that drive roll yield.

To decompose the roll yield into its basic components we need to obtain data for the cost of storage and the financing costs. Historic and current storage costs for copper can be obtained directly from the LME or from an LME broker. A chart showing average storage rates for the major base metals markets from 1998 to 2010 is shown in Exhibit 5-3. The cost of financing used in this analysis is assumed to be the three-month LIBOR, but other measures could be used without altering the key conclusions. Now that we know the roll yield plus the financing and storage costs, we can solve for the convenience yield.

The results of this analysis for the past 12 years are shown in Exhibit 5-2. The first, and most important, conclusion is that rolling a long exposure in the futures contract has been significantly better than holding physical copper. To start with, the roll yield of 1.4% means that the index-oriented investor made 1.4% on top of any spot returns. However, the benefit of owning futures

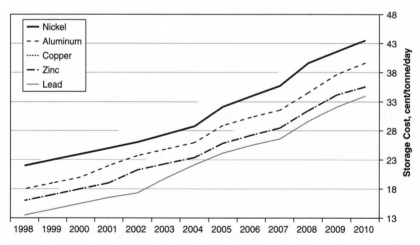

Exhibit 5-3 Base Metal Storage Costs (Cent/Tonne/Day)

Source: LME, as of December 31, 2010

versus physical inventory is generally much larger than just the benefit accruing from the roll yield. The average financing cost over this period was 3.3%, and the average storage cost was 3.1%. These are two costs that the average index investor did not have to pay, but a holder of the physical metal would have incurred. The holder of physical copper metal assigns a value to having physical copper available for commercial operations, and over the last 12 years, this convenience yield has averaged 7.8% per year. Assuming an investor wanted to gain exposure to the price of copper, using futures has had an average return advantage of 7.8% per year versus owning the physical copper metal! Just passively holding physical commodities is a very expensive alternative to the typical, futures-based commodity index–oriented investments.

To put it another way, consider the year is 1998 and two investors have the fantastic foresight to see the coming surge in Chinese commodity demand, and they each decide to take $1,000 and get exposure to the price of copper. One investor chooses to buy $1,000 worth of physical copper and store it in a warehouse. The other investor chose to invest his $1,000 in the GSCI copper subindex. The investor in the GSCI copper subindex gained financial exposure to copper prices. He held copper futures contracts to replicate the index and earned an additional yield by investing his cash in three-month T-bills. The other investor gained exposure to copper prices through the physical metal, which earned no yield and required storage costs be paid to the warehouse holding the physical copper. Both investors started by holding $1,000 of exposure to copper, but over the 13 years from 1998 to 2011, the investor who invested in the GSCI copper index would have had a total return over twice as large as the investor who owned physical copper. The investor in the GSCI copper subindex had a total return of 767%, compared to only 305% for the investor holding physical copper. This return difference is due to the convenience yield that accrues to holders of commodity futures but not to those who buy and hold the physical commodity.

APPLICATION TO PHYSICAL METAL-BACKED ETFs

Investors seeking higher commodity returns will not likely find the answer through passively investing in physical commodities. Instead, just the opposite tends to be true. The annual cost of storage combined with the zero yield from holding a physical commodity will almost certainly, over an extended period of time, result in lower returns for a physical commodity investment relative to investing in commodity index–oriented investments or futures contracts, which both can earn a convenience yield. The one exception to this rule is gold. Gold is not consumed like most commodities. It is estimated that 166,000 metric tons of gold have been mined throughout history and virtually all this gold still exists above ground in the form of jewelry, gold bars, etc. (World Gold Council, 2012) This means that the available inventory of gold is incredibly large relative to the 2,000 to 3,000 metric tons of annual physical demand from electronics and jewelry. In addition to abundant inventories, gold is very cheap to store compared with other commodities.

While base metals might cost a few percent per year to store and grains can cost upward of 10%, gold can be stored for as little as 0.1% per year because it doesn't corrode and has a high dollar value and density. (To illustrate, consider that all the gold in the world could be held in roughly 2½ Olympic-size swimming pools.) The abundance of physical inventory combined with low storage costs means the convenience yield on gold is often near zero. Consequently, in gold there is little performance difference whether an investor chooses to hold gold futures or physical gold.

As of 2011, several firms had launched or were working to launch physically backed base metals ETFs, particularly in copper, to try and replicate the success that was seen in physically backed gold ETFs. We believe investors should be aware that these new physically backed commodity ETFs have the potential to substantially underperform commodity futures–based investments. Some investors prefer the idea of holding the physical commodity because of an increased sense of security; however, an ETF, even one that owns physical commodities, is still a financial instrument that depends on the solvency of the issuing firm and functioning financial markets in order to recoup one's investment.

Another point to consider is that when investors buy a physical commodity ETF, they have given $100 of cash for every $100 of commodity exposure. However, in the case of commodity futures, investors are only required to post margin, typically on the order of several percent of the notional. In thinking about the unlikely (it is hoped) event of fraud or default by a futures exchange or the operator of an ETF, this fact should also be considered. Ultimately, each investor must consider the best investment method to achieve his or her desired commodity exposure. If physical commodity investments are utilized, then investors should make sure that the perceived benefits of physical ownership outweigh the costs of potential underperformance versus commodity futures or a commodity index.

GENERALIZING TO OTHER COMMODITIES

While the above roll yield example focused on copper, the same analysis can be conducted across the grain, base metal, and energy sectors with similar results. The convenience yield is almost always positive, and in many cases significantly so. Commodities in these sectors typically have had a convenience yield that has averaged between 5 and 15% over the past decade. In the case of the soft commodities such as coffee or sugar, data for the cost of storage vary widely; and unlike the grain markets, there is generally no definite storage rate set by the exchange. In the soft commodities, drawing detailed conclusions about the convenience yield is more difficult, but the general conclusions from other markets still apply. Convenience yields for all major commodities have been mostly positive over the last decade. This means that passively holding physical commodities, which don't receive any convenience yield, would have underperformed passive investments in commodity futures across nearly all major commodity markets.

Given the unattractiveness of holding physical commodities, some might ask, "Why does anyone hold physical commodity inventories?" Kaldor, who first coined the term *convenience yield* in a paper he wrote in the 1930s, suggested that physical inventories are held by consumers in order to minimize the "cost and trouble of ordering frequent deliveries, or of waiting for deliveries" (Kaldor, 1939). An investor or commercial participant should only hold physical inventory if the value he or she receives from holding physical inventory meets or exceeds the convenience yield.

For example, one portion of a business might agree to hold physical inventories even if it isn't economical on paper, because it allows another portion of the business to operate more efficiently and generate a greater profit. In the case of wheat, a grain company might hold wheat stocks because it has a flour milling operation that needs to be able to have a certain inventory of wheat on hand to provide a buffer against supply disruptions or an increase in orders. The cost of holding wheat stocks, even if the curve is in backwardation, is expected to be more than covered by the margins received in turning the wheat into flour. On the other hand, an investor who owns commodity exposure for reasons of diversification, inflation hedging, or price appreciation presumably receives much less, if any, benefit from holding a physical commodity like copper. Therefore, the main holders of physical commodities are typically commercial entities that receive some benefit from those physical inventories.

Another, related explanation for the existence of convenience yield comes from Keynes's theory of normal backwardation, which we first discussed in Chapter 3. According to Keynes's logic, producers are more likely to hedge their exposure than consumers; thus speculators must be incentivized to take the other side of this producer flow in order to balance the market. Speculators would not take the other side of this flow if they couldn't on average earn a return for their services. This situation results in futures' prices that trade below market expectations for future spot prices. Futures' prices trading lower than future expectations of spot prices results in a convenience yield that accrues to the speculator. In this case, the index-oriented investor would be better off holding futures-based exposure to commodities than the physical commodities themselves.

The conclusions reached by Keynes and Kaldor are very similar, but they are arrived at from completely different perspectives. Keynes's explanation of convenience yield is viewed from the perspective of a producer seeking to hedge future price risk, while Kaldor's original discussion of convenience yield viewed the issue from the perspective of the consumer or processer. In practice, it is the interaction of producer flows along with the relative economics of storage operators that determines the level of convenience yield that can accrue to holders of commodity futures.

A FURTHER DIVE INTO THE COMPONENTS OF ROLL YIELD

The prior discussion focused on the convenience yield and its role in determining the relative attractiveness of physical versus index or futures-based commodity exposure. However, the convenience yield is only important in assessing relative attractiveness, as it represents the return difference between holding physical versus futures-based commodity exposure. The roll yield (the convenience yield plus storage financing costs) is very important to the index-oriented investor because it is an absolute, not relative, measure of the investors' opportunity cost or benefit. The roll yield is the carry that a long-term investor receives or pays in a commodity index–oriented investment. Given this, it is worthwhile to consider in more detail the individual elements that make up the roll yield.

Storage Cost

Looking at Exhibit 5-2, which decomposed the roll yield of copper, notice how steady the financing and storage costs are relative to the convenience yield. This is to be expected since financing rates are driven by short-term yields, which tend to be much less volatile than commodity prices. Moreover, storage costs are often fixed, fluctuating even less than short-term rates. Instead, most of the variation in storage rates, or yields, is not due to changes in the actual storage cost, i.e., X cents per pound per month, but rather due to changes in the price of the commodity. For example, if a commodity doubles in price, the investor essentially sees the storage rate per dollar notional of the commodity get cut in half even though the cost of storage per unit of volume or weight remains the same. When a commodity is cheap or has a low price, the cost of storage on a percentage basis is high, and the overall roll yield is reduced. Similarly, when the price of a commodity is high, the cost of storage is lower, and the roll yield is increased. This means the storage rate, along with its impact on roll yield, is procyclical with the underlying price of the commodity, an effect that can become noticeable for certain high-storage-costs commodities like those in the grain markets.

Financing rates are generally similar across commodities, varying with the general cost of credit in the economy. Storage rates, on the other hand, can vary greatly among different commodities. Storage rates depend primarily upon the cost of building storage plus the cost of insuring and maintaining the grade or quality of the commodity over time. For example, the storage rate of gold is very low because it has a high dollar value and a high density. A ton of gold is worth about $50 million, whereas a ton of aluminum is worth roughly $2,000 (as of December 30, 2010). In addition, gold is over seven times as dense as aluminum. The combination of higher dollar value and density means that in a given amount of space, you can store roughly 175,000 times as much value in gold as you can in aluminum. The comparison becomes even more stark using oil or grains, which have even lower densities and lower values per unit of weight.

In terms of maintaining quality, commodities lie across a broad spectrum. Gold on the one end has almost no maintenance requirements, while some metals such as copper and steel must be stored in appropriate conditions to avoid oxidation or other damage. On the

other end of the scale, grains and petroleum products are more difficult to store and often require regular rotation to avoid degradation,
which makes them more expensive to store.

These basic, fundamental features are the dominant drivers of
storage costs. As such, the ranking of storage costs among commodities tends to be quite static over time because the costs are dependent
upon the underlying physical properties of the commodities themselves. The biggest impact to relative storage rates is just the relative
price change between commodities; e.g., the price of copper doubles
relative to that of aluminum or vice versa. Exhibit 5-4 shows the
approximate annual storage rate for 13 commodities as a percentage of the commodity price at the end of 2010. These storage costs
and their fundamental drivers should be very important to investors
because they directly impact the opportunity cost of a commodity
index–oriented investment.

Commodity	Cost of Storage, %/Year
Crude oil	6.9
Heating oil	7.5
RBOB gasoline	7.9
Gold	0.2
Silver	0.4
Copper	1.5
Aluminum	5.6
Nickel	0.9
Zinc	5.2
Lead	4.8
Corn	10.1
Soybeans	4.6
Kansas wheat	6.7

Exhibit 5-4 **Approximate Cost of Storage as a Percentage of the Commodity Price**

Source: Chicago Board of Trade, Chicago Mercantile Exchange, Kansas City Board of Trade, LME, Morgan Stanley, PIMCO, as of December 31, 2010

Convenience Yield

The final, and generally most volatile, component of roll yield is the convenience yield. The convenience yield rarely crosses below zero since physical arbitrage through buying the physical commodity and selling futures puts a theoretical floor at zero in all but extreme scenarios. On the upside, convenience yield is basically unbounded. As previously stated, convenience yield can be thought of as the value that commercial market participants assign to holding stocks of physical inventory. It is literally the cost that market participants pay to hold inventories rather than buying them at a future date. Therefore, in order to understand the drivers of convenience yield, we need to understand what drives the value placed on holding physical inventories.

Suppose inventory levels for a given commodity such as copper are very low. For many commercial participants, having insufficient supplies of copper will be unacceptable, because it may require that they shut down production, or it may lead to expensive delays in other related processes or an inability to meet customer orders. When inventories are scarce, the ability to source and guarantee future supply decreases, which increases the willingness of commercial participants to pay a premium to hold inventories of a given commodity. Similarly, when inventories are plentiful, commercial participants will be unwilling to pay a premium for storing the commodity since they have high confidence that the commodity will be readily available for purchase in the future when they need it.

Exhibit 5-5 shows the strong relationship between convenience yield and inventory levels for the copper market. Exhibit 5-6 shows a regression of convenience yields and inventory levels. Notice that the convenience yield moves asymptotically toward zero as inventories grow, while it increases exponentially as inventories decline toward zero. *At some point, inventory levels can become low enough that the convenience yield becomes larger than the storage and financing costs. When this happens, the roll yield will become positive and the curve is said to be in backwardation.* Conversely, when inventories are high,

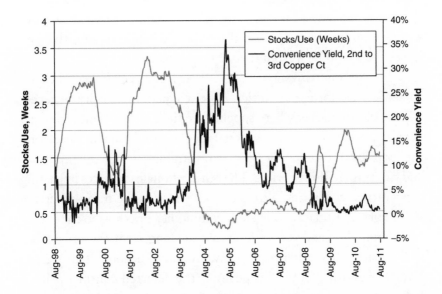

Exhibit 5-5 Convenience Yield and Inventory Levels for the Copper Market

Source: Bloomberg, PIMCO, LME, as of June 30, 2011

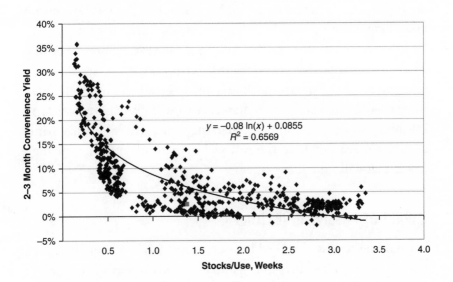

Exhibit 5-6 Convenience Yield Versus Inventory Levels for the Copper Market

Source: Bloomberg, PIMCO, LME, as of June 30, 2011

the convenience yield is generally not sufficient to offset the cost of storage and financing, and so the roll yield would be negative and the curve would be in contango.

In addition to inventory levels, other factors can impact the convenience yield for commodities. All else equal, higher prices generally indicate a market where supplies are tight or insufficient to meet demand, while lower prices signal an excess of supply. Therefore, higher prices are generally associated with higher convenience yields and vice versa for lower prices. The other rationale for prices impacting convenience yields, and ultimately roll yields, is the mean-reverting nature of real (inflation-adjusted) commodity prices. Look at almost any commodity, and you will see that the long-term real price tends to fluctuate, albeit often very widely, around some long-term average level. When the roll yield is positive, the deferred contract price is below the nearby contract price; thus the market is pricing in some degree of mean reversion from higher to lower prices. Since the market prices include forward expectations about prices through the term structure of the futures contracts, a positive roll yield when prices are high makes intuitive sense. To the extent that the mean reversion takes longer than implied by the market, the investor's returns will be enhanced from this positive roll yield. However, if prices collapse suddenly, the positive roll yield will be more than offset by negative spot returns from the decline in price. Ideally, an index-oriented investor looks to benefit from markets that will likely have long-term inventory shortages, and hence persistent positive roll yields, while avoiding markets where the roll yield is a result of transient high prices that will soon likely collapse.

IMPACT OF PASSIVE INVESTORS

It would be remiss not to address one final driver of roll yields, the naive, purely passive investor. As we have shown previously, the roll yield in commodities markets is driven very much by fundamental factors. The dominant driver of changes in roll yields across commodity markets tends to be changes in available inventory levels. This was the case before passive investors were prominent, and it is still the case today. However, just because roll yields still respond primarily to fundamental factors doesn't imply that investors have zero marginal impact.

Passive investors by design are regular sellers of the nearby contract and buyers of the deferred contract. As they became a larger share of the market from 2004 onward, they altered the supply-demand balance for rolling contracts in the futures market. In order for these investors to roll, someone else must be incentivized to take the other side of that trade. Someone else must buy the nearby contract and sell the deferred contract. Therefore, it would seem logical that for a given level of inventories, we should on average see a lower level of convenience as passive investors increase in prominence.

Exhibit 5-7 shows the same regression of convenience yields for copper that was previously shown in Exhibit 5-6, but this time

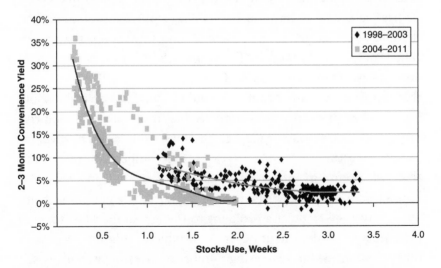

Exhibit 5-7 **Convenience Yield Versus Inventory Level, Before and After Increased Index Activity**

Source: Bloomberg, PIMCO, LME, as of June 30, 2011

the data are broken into two periods. The first period, pre-2004, represents the period where there was little index activity. The second period, from 2004 onward, represents the period of increased passive activity. The fundamentals of the market are the overriding dominant force for both time periods. When inventories of copper fell in mid–2004 and reached levels that hadn't been seen in the previous several years, the convenience yield rose exponentially to new highs, as expected. The presence of passive investors did not alter the fundamental nature of the market or the shape of the curve. However, comparing periods of similar inventory levels, i.e., stocks to use from one to two weeks, the convenience yield was on average marginally lower during the period of increased passive index activity. The same analysis shows similar results not only for the other base metals but also for energy and grain commodities.

Increased passive investment has generally resulted in lower convenience yields and therefore lower roll yields at the margin. As discussed previously, the reason for this impact is the change in the balance of supply and demand for the rolling of commodity futures. As passive investors have become a larger portion of the market, there has been an increased supply of long futures positions to be rolled forward each month. This does not mean investors should avoid investing in commodities. Commodities are still an asset class that can provide many benefits, including portfolio diversification, inflation hedging, and excess returns due to the presence of a risk premium or convenience yield in the forward curve. However, as passive investment activity increases, the competition to capture that risk premium increases. Recall Keynes's notion of normal backwardation that suggests that the forward price of a commodity will on average trade at a discount to the actual market-expected price due to the dominant nature of producer hedging. As passive investment grows, an increasing number of investors will likely sell nearby contracts and buy deferred contracts, which should lower the degree of normal backwardation and risk premium. This increasing competition to capture the risk premium in the commodities market emphasizes the importance of intelligent commodity index investing in order to maximize total return potential. The role of intelligent commodity index investing is to determine which markets have the highest risk premiums that are likely to persist, thereby providing investors with compensation for the risks they bear.

In this chapter, we introduced and then presented a detailed discussion of the concept of roll yield. We subdivided it into storage and financing costs and a convenience yield that is paid by the holder of physical inventory. As an example, we studied the case of copper and generalized this to other commodities. Finally, we applied this to the case of physical metal ETFs and also discussed the possible impact of passive index replication. Armed with this knowledge, we go further in the next chapter and discuss first how roll yield can be an important driver of long-term commodity index returns. In addition, we illustrate ways in which investors can increase the roll yield of their portfolio relative to a commodity index.

CHAPTER 6

Maximizing Roll Yield

In this chapter, we move beyond the drivers of roll yield and look at its impact on the short- and long-term returns of commodity index–oriented investments. After demonstrating the importance of roll yield in long-term commodity index returns, we look at several methods of maximizing roll yield for the intelligent commodity index–oriented investor. We do this with the help of concrete examples. In particular, we examine some of the popular systematic strategies currently implemented by commodity trading desks and often offered to investors for a fee under names such as "dynamic" or "optimized" roll yield indexes. We decompose these strategies into the individual components of roll yield that we discussed in the previous chapter, namely, financing costs, storage costs, and convenience yield. This decomposition helps facilitate a more thorough understanding of the fundamental drivers of the relative returns of these types of strategies. This type of analysis should further reinforce the roll yield as a dominant driver of long-term returns for the different commodity sectors, and it should also allow readers the expertise to construct their own fundamental-based roll yield optimization strategies.

ROLL YIELD AS A DRIVER OF LONG-TERM RETURNS

As discussed previously, the investor's return from the commodity futures portion of a commodity index–oriented investment is conventionally referred to as the *excess return*. This distinguishes it from the *total return*, which also includes the return on the collateral portfolio. The excess return can be decomposed into two pieces: the spot price return and the roll yield return. Over short horizons, i.e., within one to two years, the excess returns in individual commodities and indexes tend to be dominated by the spot price returns, which incorporate the changes in expectations discussed in Chapter 3. We believe this is sensible because most of the 20 or so commodities that make up the DJUBSCI or S&P GSCI have annual price volatilities in the 20–40% range, substantially larger than the average annual roll yield of most commodities.

Exhibit 6-1 shows the excess return, spot return, and roll yield returns for 2010 for the 24 commodities that make up the S&P GSCI. As expected, over a one-year horizon the spot returns largely dominate the roll yield in determining excess return. In any given year, the roll yield tells you very little about the excess return. Statistically, consider that the correlation between the annual spot price returns and the annual excess returns of these 24 commodities was 96% for 2010, while the correlation between the annual roll yields and excess returns was only 39%. Therefore, the roll yield is likely to be of secondary importance to overall performance for speculative or trend-following commodity traders that typically hold positions for short periods of time.

Index-oriented investors, however, follow a very different investment approach to that of most trend followers or speculative traders. The objective of index-oriented investors is typically either to gain exposure to commodities in order to hedge against future inflation surprises or to diversify their portfolios. As a result of these objectives, index-oriented investors typically have a longer-term investment horizon, and their commodity exposure is predominantly

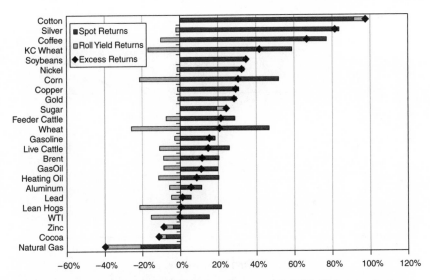

Exhibit 6-1 Breakdown of Returns into Spot and Roll Yield Components for the 24 Commodities That Make Up the S&P GSCI for 2010

Source: Bloomberg, Standard & Poor's, PIMCO, as of December 31, 2010

long-only. Here the returns from roll yields become increasingly important.

As Exhibit 6-1 shows, the excess returns in 2010 were primarily driven by the spot price movements of each individual commodity, but is this still true over a multiyear period? It turns out that the driver of excess returns shifts from spot returns to roll yield over progressively longer time periods. To visually demonstrate this shift, Exhibit 6-2 shows the annualized excess returns regressed against the annualized roll yield for a sample of 19 commodities from 1994 to 2010 (regression is for the 19 commodities that were published S&P GSCI subindexes as of 1994). The correlation between the excess returns and roll yields of these 19 commodities is a whopping 94%!

Over this same period, the correlation between excess and spot returns was only 61% (see Exhibit 6-3). The relative importance of spot price returns and roll yield returns is flipped when one goes

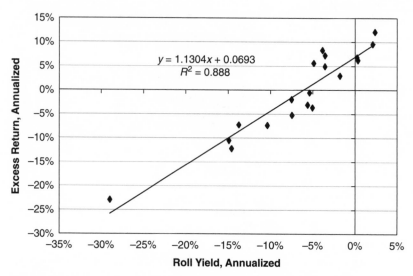

Exhibit 6-2 Excess Return Versus Roll Yield from 1994 to 2010 for 19 Commodities in the S&P GSCI.

Source: Bloomberg, Standard & Poor's, PIMCO, as of December 31, 2010

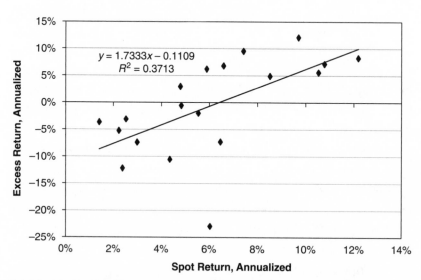

Exhibit 6-3 Excess Returns Versus Spot Return from 1994 to 2010 for 19 Commodities in the S&P GSCI

Source: Bloomberg, Standard & Poor's, PIMCO, as of December 31, 2010

from shorter time horizons to longer time horizons. This means that for an investor looking at commodities as an asset class and part of a longer-term investment, the first priority should be to seek to maximize the roll yield. The methods of achieving this, essentially seeking to further enhance the positive roll yield offered by certain commodities while minimizing the drag from commodities with negative roll yield, will be explored at length throughout the remainder of this chapter.

While it may seem counterintuitive that roll yield is so important, it is the result of the compounding effect of roll yield's often persistent year-after-year impact versus the mean-reverting nature of spot commodity prices (when measured in real terms over very long time horizons). This is an effect that is familiar to bond market investors in the sense that a portfolio with positive carry and roll-down produces a tailwind for returns. This tailwind can help a portfolio outperform its benchmark in the long run, even though interest rate and price movements tend to dominate short-term performance. Similarly, studies (Arnott, 2003) have shown that the historical long-term performance of equities has been primarily attributable to the dividend yield. In any one year, the return received from dividends is likely to be dwarfed by outright changes in the price of the stock, but over time their cumulative impact is enormous. This compounding effect that is observed in equities and bonds is no different in the commodity markets.

Consider a hypothetical example of two commodities, Commodity A and Commodity B. Assume that for some reason Commodity B has an annual roll yield that can be expected to be 10% below Commodity A on average. Fifteen years from now, an investor looks back and sees that Commodity A had a roll yield on average of 0% per year, while Commodity B had a roll yield of −10% per year. If the spot price of Commodity A remained unchanged, then Commodity B's spot price would need to increase by 10% per year for the excess returns of A and B to be identical. This means the spot price of Commodity B would need to increase by a total of 317%.

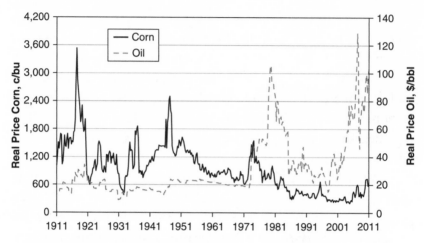

Exhibit 6-4 Long-Term Real Commodity Prices, WTI Crude Oil and Corn

Source: Bloomberg, Haver, Morgan Stanley, as of March 1, 2012

The longer the horizon is, the more unlikely it is that Commodity B could outperform Commodity A. In any given year, Commodity B may outperform Commodity A, but over a sufficiently long time frame, it will almost surely lose.

Exhibit 6-4 shows the long-term real prices of oil and corn over the past 100 years, and Exhibit 6-5 shows the long-term real prices for gold and copper over the same time period. While there can certainly be spot price moves of 500–600% over a few-year period, the overall level of inflation-adjusted prices has been fairly stable. Over the past 100-year period, the total annualized percent changes in the real price for oil, corn, copper, and gold have been 1.8%, −0.6%, 0.3%, and 1.2%, respectively. While there is not accurate data on roll yield for the past 100 years, these long-term price movements are generally modest compared to the roll yield returns of recent years. From 1994 to 2010 roll yield for 19 different commodities ranged from −30 to +3% (see Exhibit 6-2). Looking forward, if we extrapolate from this recent period, roll yields could be substantially more important to long-term investor returns than spot price movements.

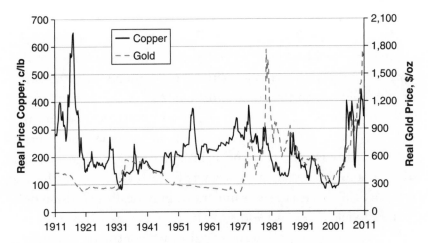

Exhibit 6-5 Long-Term Real Commodity Prices, Gold and Copper

Source: Bloomberg, Haver, Morgan Stanley, as of March 1, 2012

If an investor wants to maximize the excess returns from a long-only basket of commodities over an extended time horizon, it is unlikely to do much good to pick the long-term winners in terms of spot prices. Instead, such an investor needs to select the commodities that are going to have a strong positive roll yield. However, the roll yield returns aren't known a priori any more than future spot price moves are. Both the spot and roll yield returns are dependent upon many fundamental factors and future developments, most of which are not foreseeable many years out. Hence it is important to develop a fundamental framework based on the supply-demand balance and storage costs that allows one to have a view on roll yields. It is this framework that we attempt to flesh out in this chapter.

SEEKING TO MAXIMIZE ROLL YIELD

Given the importance of roll yield in long-term commodity index returns, many potential solutions for maximizing it have been proposed. The most common method, and the primary method underlying many more complicated strategies, is what is known as the *optimized roll yield* strategy. Whether talking about a single commodity or a basket of commodities, the basic premise of the optimized roll yield strategy is the same—always hold the commodity contract on the point of the curve with the best roll yield.

For example, assume that the front-month contract on the crude oil curve is the January contract, and assume that its price is $100. Also assume that the February contract has a price of $100.50 and the rest of the contracts from March onward have a price of $100. Such a curve is illustrated graphically in Exhibit 6-6. The roll yields are −0.5% for the January contract, 0.5% for the February contract, and zero for all other contracts. According to the optimized roll yield strategy, an investor should hold the February contract since it has the best roll yield. While this might seem illogical and even risky given that the February contract appears so rich relative to the rest of the curve, it highlights the basic nature of the optimized roll yield strategy. The optimized roll yield strategy works best when the shape of the curve remains unchanged and forward prices are not realized.

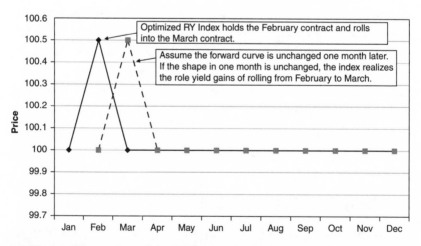

Exhibit 6-6 Illustration of the Mechanics for an Optimized Roll Yield Strategy. Sample for Illustrative Purposes Only.

If the curve shape remains unchanged, then by definition the dislocation at the second month of the curve persists. In this case, holding a long position in the second contract and each month rolling into the third contract is the best trade, because with every roll that passes, a 0.5% roll yield profit is realized. The risk is obviously that the investor moves into the second contract, but the dislocation proves short lived and goes away while the investor still holds the second contract. Exhibit 6-7 shows an illustration of such an example. In this case, the second contract on the curve underperforms all other contracts in spot terms, and there is no longer any roll yield advantage between different contracts. In this case, the optimized roll yield strategy earned the investor a $0.50 loss.

Taking this example one step further, if the second contract declined by more than $0.50, then the second contract would at that time have the worst roll yield on the curve, and the front contract would have the best roll yield. At this point, the second contract would again appear mispriced relative to the rest of the curve. However, the "logic" of the optimized roll yield strategy would have an investor move out of the second contract into the

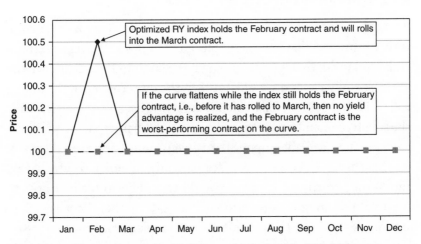

Exhibit 6-7 **Illustration of the Risks in an Optimized Roll Yield Strategy When the Forward Curve Changes. Sample for Illustrative Purposes Only.**

front contract, thereby locking in the loss from what might have been a temporary spot move. This example is quite simplistic, but it is useful in demonstrating the mechanics and potential shortcomings of a naive optimized roll yield strategy.

This optimized roll yield strategy can also be applied to a basket of commodities. This is the basic premise behind most of the optimized roll yield indexes or strategies that one hears of. In this case, an investor would look at the current roll yield across a basket of commodities and then go long some subset of those with the highest roll yield, say the top 50%. To be clear, such an approach does not ensure that an investor will achieve the best excess returns, nor does it guarantee exposure across a desired set of commodities. If the forward prices of commodity curves are realized, then roll yield gains will be exactly offset by spot price losses. As previously stated, the underlying assumption of the optimized roll yield strategy is that the shape of the commodity curve remains unchanged. To the extent this assumption is true, then an optimized roll yield strategy should outperform.

DISSECTING THE OPTIMIZED ROLL YIELD

The optimized roll yield approach has a rationale that on the surface is very intuitive. The logic is simple: if the long-run driver of returns is the roll yield, then you should own the commodities that have the greatest roll yield and should not own the ones that have the lowest roll yield. In addition, if a market is currently backwardated, it means the supply-demand balance is tight. In a tight market, there is risk of a stockout; i.e., available supplies of a given commodity are exhausted. In this case, prices must rise dramatically in order to effectively ration the remaining supply. It would seem logical for investors to want to have long exposure to such a tight market, because when inventories are low, the probability of a sudden price increase rises. Therefore, not only do investors have exposure to potential upside price spikes, but they can also capture a positive roll yield while waiting for these price spikes. Similar logic applies to a market in contango. The supply-demand balance is loose; inventories are either high or rising. An investor doesn't want exposure to a market that is oversupplied and therefore structurally weak. After all, who wants to own something when there will be even more of it in the future? The investor then is uninterested in contango markets not only because they have poor roll yield but also because they have little potential for spot price appreciation. If only it were that easy!

The argument against a naive mechanical or rule-based opti-mized roll yield approach is that all markets regularly shift from back-wardation to contango and vice versa; hence it is important to not run the strategy on autopilot. When a market is tight and in backward-ation, the price of the nearby contracts is higher than the price of the more deferred contracts. Eventually the price becomes high enough that more supply is introduced or enough demand is destroyed, and the market moves from a deficit to a surplus. When this happens, the shape of the commodity curve moves from backwardation to contango, often violently and in a very short time. Instead of making a 10 or 20% return over the next year from the positive roll yield, prices may fall by two or more times that amount in weeks or months. Instead of making a nice return from the positive roll yield, investors are left with large losses from spot price declines. In addition, after such price declines, the curve has likely shifted into contango, and the investors now hold a commodity with a negative roll yield, but the reason that they bought the commodity in the first place was to capture the positive roll yield. An optimized roll yield–type strategy like the one discussed above often results in the investor buying when prices are high and selling after prices have collapsed.

THE REAL SECRET BEHIND ROLL YIELD

In truth, it turns out that optimizing the roll yield and assuming that forward curves will not be realized does tend to do a good job of improving the excess returns of standard commodity indexes.

However, as we will explore in more detail later, *the reason the optimized roll yield approach has generally outperformed has less to do with the notion of picking the "right" commodities with tight supply and demand fundamentals and more to do with just being a good filter for selecting commodities with lower storage costs.* In the following pages, we walk through specifics regarding the construction and attribution of returns for an optimized roll yield strategy to more completely understand why this strategy has often outperformed more traditional, less dynamic commodity indexes such as the DJUBSCI or S&P GSCI.

We construct an optimized roll yield strategy by computing the roll yield between the first and second contract for each of the 24 different commodities in the S&P GSCI (in general, we use a contract roll schedule similar to that of the S&P GSCI) at the end of each month. The 12 commodities that have the best roll yield at the end of each month make up the holdings for the upcoming month. In technical terms, each month the optimized roll yield strategy is composed of the commodities that had an above-median roll yield on the last month's end. The commodities are all assumed to be equally weighted. To serve as a benchmark for the optimized roll yield strategy, we have also constructed a hypothetical index that is an equally weighted basket of the 24 commodities that make up the S&P GSCI. We also compute an equally weighted basket for the half of the commodities that had a below-median roll yield. Exhibit 6-8 shows the performance for each of these three hypothetical indexes since 2000. Prior to 2000, the universe of commodities with reliable data starts to diminish, and we believe this 11-year sample gives a reasonable weighting between the data before and after commodity index–oriented investment gained widespread popularity.

At first glance, it seems this optimized roll yield strategy would be extremely efficient at maximizing excess returns by ensuring investors benefit from the long-run driver of returns, roll yield. However, before reaching such a conclusion, it is worthwhile to decompose the excess returns of each index into both a spot and roll yield component.

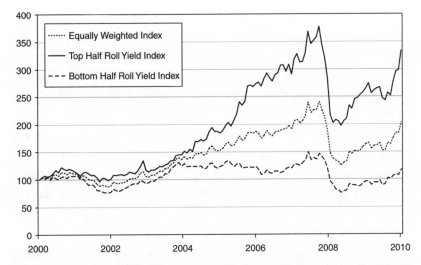

Exhibit 6-8   Comparison of Performance Between High and Low Roll Yield Commodities Relative to an Equally Weighted Portfolio

Source: Bloomberg, Standard & Poor's, PIMCO, as of December 31, 2010

	Equally Weighted Index	Top Half Roll Yield Index	Bottom Half Roll Yield Index
Excess Return	7.73%	12.61%	2.85%
Roll Yield Return	−7.73%	5.42%	−20.87%
Spot Return	15.46%	7.20%	23.72%

Exhibit 6-9   Excess Returns of High and Low Roll Yield Commodities Deconstructed into Both a Spot and Roll Yield Component

As shown in Exhibit 6-9, the optimized roll yield strategy clearly had a superior excess return. From the exhibit, it is apparent that the driver of these superior excess returns was the substantially better roll yield for the commodities with an above-median roll yield. The roll yield for the optimized roll yield strategy averaged 5.42%, which is over 25 percentage points better than the roll yield of the commodities with the lowest roll yields. This exhibit implies that if a commodity had a good roll yield in the prior month, it would likely continue to have a good roll yield over the next month. However, the less positive part of these results is found in the row showing spot returns. Notice that the spot returns for the optimized roll yield strategy were far below the returns for the other indexes, averaging just 7.2% versus 15.46% for the equally weighted basket. This means that the commodities with the best roll yields were increasing in price at a below-average pace compared with the commodity complex on the whole. Since the spot returns of the optimized roll yield strategy lagged those of the broad market, a large portion of the potential roll yield returns were not actually being realized because they were being offset with spot price losses. This underperformance in spot returns is a result of the buying-high, selling-low effect that we outlined previously and is one potential risk of systematic roll yield strategies.

The optimized roll yield approach illustrated above holds the commodities that had the best roll yield in the prior month. Since storage costs and financing costs are fairly constant, in any given month the optimized roll yield approach likely holds the commodities with a relatively high convenience yield. Recall from the previous chapter that the convenience yield is inversely correlated with inventories but positively correlated with the price of the commodity. Therefore, by dynamically switching into the commodities with the highest roll yields, the optimized roll yield strategy is switching into the commodities that have already had relatively large spot price moves. This results in investors buying in at the top when the roll yield is good only to sell the position after the price falls.

Upon drilling down into the holdings of the optimized roll yield strategy, some curious patterns are observed with how frequently the various commodities and commodity sectors are each held. One way to identify such anomalies is to look at the percentage of time that each commodity has a roll yield above the median roll yield for all commodities. It might be expected that all the commodities are in the upper half of overall roll yields roughly half of the time and in the lower half of roll yields the other half of the time. However, corn is in the upper half of roll yields only 6% of the time over the whole period. Similarly, wheat is in the upper half of roll yields only 11% of the time. Nickel is in the upper half 97% of the time. In fact, the least frequently held metal turns out to be zinc, at 54%, while the most frequently held grain is soybeans at 51%. This means that every single metal is held more often than even the most frequently held grain. In addition, it turns out that these same themes are true even if you break the full period studied into smaller three- or five-year subperiods. Why should this be the case? Why does a strategy that seeks to hold the most backwardated half of the commodity universe virtually always end up holding nickel and almost never holding corn?

Recall the previous chapter discussing the drivers of roll yield. The drivers of roll yield were financing rates, storage rates, and convenience yields. The financing rates are similar across all commodities, and so we can ignore this component for relative roll yield differences between commodities. The convenience yield was shown to have a strong negative correlation to inventory levels. Nickel inventories fluctuated from very high to very low multiple times during this period, and yet nickel was in the upper half of roll yields 97% of the time. And so while convenience yields clearly impact the level of roll yields, they are unable to explain why metals were held with significantly higher frequencies than grains.

This only leaves storage costs to explain the anomalous pattern of why some commodities are held more frequently than others. As discussed previously, metals have a relatively low cost of storage because they are dense and can be stored indefinitely with minimal maintenance. Grains, on the other hand, are relatively expensive to store because they require more space and can spoil more easily than many other commodities. Oil and petroleum products generally sit somewhere between metals and grains in terms of storage costs. In principle, the optimized roll yield strategy is supposed to dynamically shift to the markets with the best roll yield because roll yields are both the long-run driver of returns and also a signal of market tightness. However, the optimized roll yield strategy is not as dynamic as might be imagined, and its selection of which commodities to hold appears to have less to do with changing market conditions like inventory levels and more to do with the storage cost for a given commodity.

Exhibit 6-10 shows the percentage of time that each commodity has a roll yield in the top half of all the commodities along the x axis and the average storage cost for each commodity along the y axis. The correlation between the two is striking. This demonstrates that storage costs are a dominant, structural driver of relative roll yield differences. As shown in the last chapter, the convenience yield

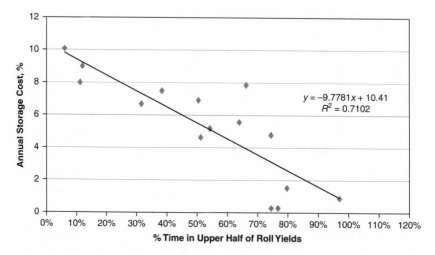

Exhibit 6-10 Time Spent in the Upper Half of the Roll Yield Basket Versus Storage Costs for the Commodities in the S&P GSCI

Note: This exhibit uses the same set of 24 commodities in the GSCI, starting in 2000, that were discussed previously. However, it excludes highly seasonal commodities such as meats and natural gas because of the distortions introduced by roll yield seasonality. Softs are also excluded because storage cost data are much more variable than for grains, metals, and energy, where costs are more uniform and observable.

Source: Bloomberg, Standard & Poor's, PIMCO

tends to be the most volatile component of the roll yield. At any given time, the convenience yield can dictate which commodities have the highest roll yield, but over the long run, these large swings in the convenience yield tend to average out since the convenience yield depends to some extent on spot prices, which tend to mean-revert. Sometimes the convenience yield will provide a large positive contribution to the roll yield, and other times the convenience yield may be near zero; but on the whole, the convenience yield tends to be less important than the persistent impact of storage costs. In a way, this shouldn't be that surprising. It fits with the familiar wisdom conveyed in the story of the tortoise and the hare, and it is the exact pattern observed with long-term commodity index returns. In the short run, the spot price returns (the hare) are the major driver of excess returns; but over an extended time frame, it is the persistent benefit or drag from roll yield (the tortoise) that will ultimately dominate excess returns.

STOCK-BASED COMMODITIES VERSUS FLOW-BASED COMMODITIES

While storage costs explain the majority of roll yield differences between commodities over long periods of time, commodities can exhibit differences in roll yield due to structural, persistent differences in convenience yield. The most common example of differences in convenience yield results from whether the supply of a commodity is more stock based (examples are grains and precious metals) or more flow based (examples are oil and base metals).

Consider the difference between the oil and corn markets. The oil market is more flow based; supply and demand are roughly in line throughout the year, and inventories provide a short-term buffer to equilibrate modest seasonal differences in supply and demand. Corn, by contrast, is a stock- or inventory-based market. There are really only two major supplies of corn that are brought to market each year, one during the northern hemisphere harvest and the other during the southern hemisphere harvest. Demand does not follow the same seasonal pattern that supply does. As such, corn must be stored throughout the year in order to allow the supply to be metered out to meet future demand. Often markets that have dominant price-based seasonality tend to be stock or inventory based, while markets without seasonality are often flow based. Stock-based markets also can be distinguished because they usually have very large storage infrastructure relative to demand, while flow-based markets are associated with more hand-to-mouth–type consumption.

Whether a market is more stock or flow based has significant implications for the behavior of convenience yield. In the case of stock-based markets, the probability of running out of a given commodity is not constant. It tends to be low for most of the year, with all the risk concentrated right before the next supply is available, e.g. the next harvest period in the case of agricultural commodities. In stock-based markets, inventories are typically comfortable most of the year, which means that convenience yields tend to be very low most of the year. However, the period where there is a risk of running out of a stock-based commodity typically sees very high convenience yields. Part of this is due to an embedded risk premium in the market as the risk of running out of the commodity is generally unacceptable, and so end users pay a premium to lock in supply at these critical times. The other reason for high convenience yields during periods of low supply is that when a shortage does occur, the price spike is often extreme, as demand is often quite price inelastic. Therefore, in stock-based markets, the convenience yield tends to be on average relatively low, with very large but infrequent spikes upward. These spikes are typically short lived and the result of a short-term inability of current inventories to meet demand.

Flow-based markets don't have large seasonal periods of high or adequate inventories, and they tend to not have storage capacity to accommodate high inventory levels. As such, they can be expected to have on average higher levels of convenience yields than stock-based markets throughout most of the year. In addition, flow-based markets often have supply shortages that exist longer than stock-based markets because they lack the large one-off supply events such as an annual harvest that can quickly rebalance stock-based markets. Due to these factors, the convenience yields in flow-based markets tend to exhibit a more persistent nature than those in stock-based markets, where supply-demand balances get reset on a regular basis.

To illustrate the difference in roll yield between stock- and flow-based markets, we have reconstructed Exhibit 6-10 to create Exhibit 6-11, where we show storage cost versus the percentage of time a commodity is in the upper half of the overall roll yields, but now we have separated the commodities in the S&P GSCI into a stock-based group and a flow-based group. Interestingly, when we split the data into stock- and flow-based groups, the results are exactly as expected. The stock-based markets typically have lower roll yields than the flow-based markets, even after controlling for

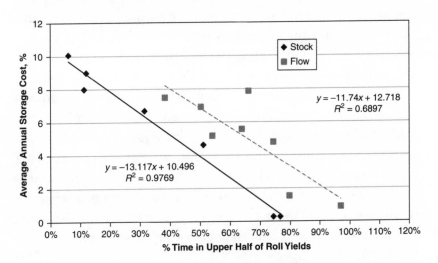

Exhibit 6-11 Time Spent in the Upper Half of the Roll Yield Basket Versus Storage Costs for the Commodities in the S&P GSCI, with Commodities Broken into Stock- and Flow-Based Groups

Source: Bloomberg, Standard & Poor's, PIMCO, as of December 31, 2010

storage cost differences. Also interestingly, for stock-based markets the correlation between the storage cost and the frequency of being in the upper half of roll yields was 0.99. This is somewhat to be expected since stock-based markets almost by definition tend to have comfortable levels of inventories and low convenience yields throughout most of the year.

While spot returns from commodities are very important since they produce the inflation hedging and diversification benefits that can make commodities attractive to investors, roll yield is equally important as the long-run driver of commodity index returns. In this chapter, we have analyzed an optimized roll yield strategy and shown it can generate above-average returns compared with an equally weighted index. We also demonstrated a strong link between the level of storage costs for various commodities and the frequency with which they are held by an optimized roll yield strategy.

This overlap between the optimized roll yield strategy and commodities with low storage costs can be used to create a simpler index with many of the positive features found in a dynamic optimized roll yield strategy. We will discuss the details of such a low-storage-cost index in greater detail in Chapter 13, but for now we just highlight that a low-storage-cost index has the advantage of holding a relatively constant basket of commodities over time as relative storage costs change infrequently. Since storage costs are fairly constant and are known a priori, we believe that a low-storage-cost index should be the baseline by which the performance of commodities as an asset class should be measured. A low-storage-cost index can also serve as a very attractive baseline for other index enhancements or trading strategies that can be developed.

In this chapter, we have discussed one of the most important factors that drive long-term commodity index returns—roll yields. This is the first thing an intelligent long-term investor should attempt to maximize, similar to a fixed-income investor looking to maximize the carry of the portfolio. The carry or roll yield can be maximized, not by investing in riskier securities, but by understanding the fundamental reasons behind the shape of commodities futures curves and using this knowledge in an attempt to outperform the index. In the next few chapters, we discuss other structural and persistent sources of returns in the commodity markets, such as seasonal strategies, substitution strategies, and option-based or volatility strategies.

CHAPTER 7

Calendar Spreads and Seasonal Strategies

In the last chapter, we discussed the long-term advantage of optimizing the roll yield of a commodity portfolio. However, to fully optimize the roll yield involves a combination of picking the right commodities and picking the right spots on those commodity futures curves. In the last chapter, we discussed a framework for this first issue of selecting the right commodities. In this chapter, we focus on the second issue of selecting the optimal point on each commodity curve by understanding different calendar and seasonal strategies across the various commodity markets. The calendar and seasonal strategies discussed in this chapter try to gain exposure at different points on the futures curve in an effort to capture risk premiums due to real or perceived supply-demand imbalances as well as segmentation among the preferred maturities for buyers and sellers.

Several commodities have distinct seasonal patterns to either their production, consumption, or both. Think of grains that have planting and harvest seasons, gasoline demand during the summer driving season, or heating oil and natural gas demand during the winter months as opposed to the summer months. Seasonal markets such as these often price in a risk premium to ensure sufficient supplies throughout the year. Understanding and exploiting these risk premiums is the key to a successful seasonal strategy. Following the calendar spreads between different months of a given commodity can also give subtle hints about market positioning as well as insights into changes in the tightness or looseness of the physical inventory situation. After all, the futures curve for any commodity is a combination of the market's expectations for the spot price of that commodity in the future plus some level of embedded risk premium. In this chapter, we will look at different examples of calendar spreads in order to illustrate how investors can potentially profit by understanding to what extent particular calendar spreads are driven by expected spot price changes or by the level of embedded risk premium (from here on, we will talk somewhat interchangeably of calendar and seasonal strategies).

Calendar spreads consist of a long position in one contract and a short position in another contract of the same commodity. As explained in the chapters on roll yield, the difference in price between any two contracts in the same commodity is a function of financing and storage costs plus the convenience yield. Therefore, any time investors put on a calendar spread, they are expressing a view about one of those three factors changing. For example, the introduction of a variable storage rate in the July 2010 Chicago soft red wheat futures contract was one classic example of a storage price change that resulted in very substantial calendar spread moves. However, material changes in the absolute level of storage costs are relatively infrequent. Typically calendar spread trades look to profit from changes in the convenience yield since this is the most volatile component of the roll yield. However, the convenience yield is just a catchall term for the portion of the roll yield not explained by the financing or roll yield components. Recalling the analysis from prior chapters, the convenience yield is directly related to factors such as inventory levels, the level of spot prices, and the risk premium embedded in the curve as a result of effects like Keynes's notion of normal backwardation. Therefore, trading and understanding calendar spreads involves taking into account these various factors.

A CRUDE OIL EXAMPLE

As a starting point, look at the crude oil curve shown in Exhibit 7-1. The front of the curve is in a strong contango for the first several months. That contango slowly moderates over the next several months and eventually shifts to a very mild backwardation for the next few years. In crude oil, like most other markets, the shape of the curve shows a strong relation to the level of inventories. In order for the curve to shift from contango to backwardation as the market was forecasting, the overall level of inventories in crude oil will likely need to decline. As inventories decline, the risk of a shortage or insufficient supplies grows, and the convenience yield rises. This is the baseline scenario that the crude oil market seemed to be predicting with the shape of the forward curve shown in Exhibit 7-1.

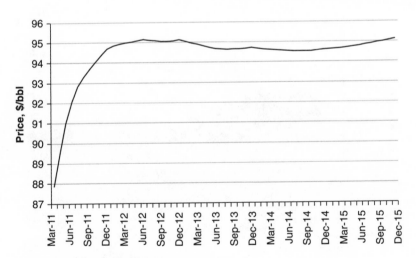

Exhibit 7-1 WTI Crude Oil Futures Curve

Source: Bloomberg, as of January 24, 2011

One example of a simple approach to assess value in the crude oil futures curve is to map the shape of the curve to a fundamental, observable factor such as the level of inventories. For example, the shape of the curve from March 2012 to April 2012 is nearly flat, and hence the roll yield is near zero. Assuming crude oil storage costs remain constant at roughly 50 cents a month, the annual storage rate is approximately 6.5% per year. Assuming a 1% financing rate, then the annual storage and financing costs are roughly 7.5% per year. This means that the convenience yield would have to be roughly 7.5% in one year in order to give a roll yield near 0%.

The historic relationship between oil inventories in the Midwest (PADD II, which contains the delivery points for WTI crude oil) and convenience yield is shown in Exhibit 7-2. On average, the convenience yield is nearly zero for stock levels above 75 million barrels, and it rises to roughly 7.5% when inventory levels fall to 70 million barrels. Thus, an interpretation of the crude oil futures curve in Exhibit 7-2 is that inventory levels in the PADD II region of the United States, shown in Exhibit 7-3, are forecast to decline from their current level of 99 million barrels to a level of roughly

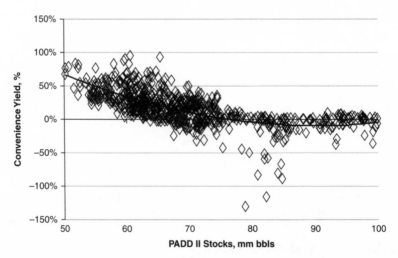

Exhibit 7-2 Convenience Yield in Oil Futures Versus PADD II Oil Inventories

Source: Bloomberg, Department of Energy, as of December 31, 2010

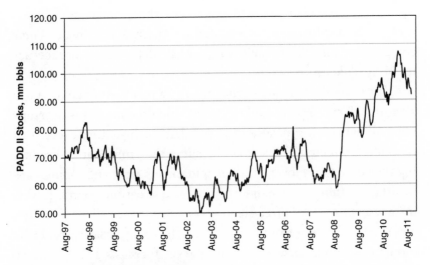

Exhibit 7-3 PADD II Oil Inventories

Source: Bloomberg, Department of Energy, PIMCO, as of December 31, 2010

70 million barrels over the next year. Any further reduction in stocks would lead to a more backwardated curve than the market currently forecasts, while stock levels above 70 million barrels would likely result in the curve staying in contango. If market participants expected that inventories would be 70 million barrels in a year, then the forward roll yield from March to April 2012 could be said to be fair. However, if market participants believed inventories would be 80 million barrels in one year's time, then the forward roll yield is more positive than expectations of future inventory levels would suggest it should be.

One possible reason for the roll yield being more positive (i.e., the curve being more backwardated) than expectations of inventories would suggest is the existence of a risk premium in the forward prices. One potential cause for such a risk premium to exist might be due to more producer than consumer hedging, creating the effect that Keynes termed *normal backwardation*. For example, if there were an imbalance in flows due to a large amount of producer hedging, then speculators or investors would need to be incentivized to take the other side of the producer hedging in order to balance the market. In exchange for their services, the speculators or investors would need to be compensated for the risk they bear. Their compensation is reflected in the form of a risk premium that accrues to the speculator or investor.

The above example of crude oil and a moderating contango is a natural shape for commodity curves when the market is oversupplied. The market typically forecasts that the inventory excess will normalize, which will result in the curve flattening out and reducing the contango. However, when a market is tight and supplies are insufficient to meet demand, the opposite situation occurs. In this instance, the curve is often steepest, and hence the roll yield is often greatest, in the very front months, and the backwardation typically moderates going forward as the market forecasts the inventory shortage will normalize. Exhibit 7-4 shows the crude oil curve as of March 2008, shortly after prices rose through $100/barrel. This is an example of the type of curve we just described. Here the roll yield is greatest at the front of the curve in the contract that most published indexes hold.

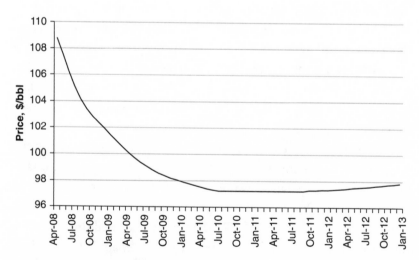

Exhibit 7-4 **WTI Crude Oil Futures Curve**

Source: Bloomberg, as of March 11, 2008

CALENDAR SPREADS HAVE A DIRECTIONAL BIAS

In practice, while the trading of commodity spreads has a significant amount to do with the future path of inventories, the future path of spot prices also has a very large impact. The reason for this is that the price volatility in a given commodity tends to increase as the time to maturity of the contract decreases. A crude oil contract with delivery in one month is obviously much more affected by the announcement of a refinery outage or a shipping disruption in Nigeria than a contract one year out. Since the front most contracts tend to have greater volatility, the spread between two contracts tends to have a directional bias consistent with the direction of the more nearby futures contract.

For example, if an investor were long March 2012 WTI versus short March 2013 WTI, this spread would tend to have a bullish bias as the investor is long the more volatile nearby contract. If prices rise, they will likely rise by more in the front than in the back, and the investor will make money. However, if prices fall, they will likely fall more in the front than in the back, and the investor will lose money. Therefore, a spread that involves being long a nearby futures contract and short a deferred futures contract is often referred to as a *bull spread* because its movement is often correlated with an outright bullish position in the commodity, while a spread that involves being short the nearby futures contract and long the deferred contract is referred to as a *bear spread*.

SHIFTED INDEX STRATEGIES

Over the past few years, the most popular calendar strategies in index investor portfolios have been bear spreads, in one form or another, because of their remarkably consistent positive returns. The most common examples of such bear spread strategies are shifted versions of the major indexes like the DJUBSCI and S&P GSCI. A shifted index on the DJUBSCI is identical to the regular DJUBSCI except that the shifted index holds contracts that are further out the curve.

For example, the two-month shifted DJUBSCI holds the contract that the regular DJUBSCI will hold in two months' time; e.g., in January the DJUBSCI will hold the March WTI crude oil futures contract, but the two-month shifted index will hold the May WTI futures contract. There are shifted indexes published by Dow Jones and S&P all the way from one to five months out the curve.

Exhibit 7-5 shows the difference in monthly returns between the two-month shifted DJUBSCI and the regular DJUBSCI. The two-month shifted index has regularly outperformed the regular DJUBSCI. From 1995 to 2004, prior to the strong growth in index investment, the average monthly difference in returns between the shifted and regular DJUBSCI was 0.15%. The reason that the shifted index outperformed is because it captures a larger amount of the risk premium present in the commodity futures curves. According to Keynes's theory of normal backwardation, producer hedging causes a risk premium to be embedded in the commodity futures curve because speculators need to receive an incentive to take the

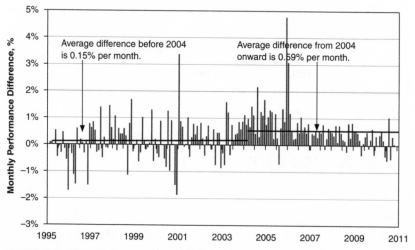

Exhibit 7-5 Monthly Performance Difference Between the Two-Month Shifted DJUBSCI and the Regular DJUBSCI

Source: Bloomberg, Dow-Jones, PIMCO, as of December 31, 2010

other side of producer hedging flows. Producers hedge along the entire curve, but the majority of their activity is in longer-dated contracts. Therefore, by moving out of the front contract, the shifted index captures a larger amount of this risk premium.

From 2004 onward, the two-month shifted index regularly outperformed the DJUBSCI by a much wider margin than historically had been the case. The average outperformance of the two-month shifted index averaged 0.59% per month, nearly a fourfold increase over the prior period. There are many possible explanations for this divergence in performance that appeared in 2004. One possibility is that producer hedging activity increased, which resulted in a larger risk premium in longer-maturity contracts. Another possibility is that the market was pricing in a drawdown in inventories, which would cause curves to move from contango to backwardation. When these inventory drawdowns failed to materialize, the forward curves were not realized, and investors were able to capture the consistently better roll yields available further out the curve.

Since inventories serve to buffer imbalances in supply and demand and reduce price volatility, the typical pattern in most commodity markets is to see prices rise as the level of inventories decline. However, this typical pattern was not observed in oil from 2004 to 2008. Over this period OECD (Organisation for Economic Co-operation and Development) oil inventories increased from 51 days of demand in 2004 to 56 days of demand in July 2008 when oil prices peaked. Perhaps some of the increase in OECD inventories was a result of growing emerging market demand combined with little oil storage availability in emerging markets. Regardless of the reason, the crude oil futures curve was in a slowly moderating contango over most of the period from 2004 to 2008, and it was pricing in some decline in inventories that continually failed to materialize. If the forward curve had mispriced oil inventories the other way, always expecting inventories to build but regularly failing to do so, it is entirely possible we could have a different version of history where shifted indexes underperformed the normal index over an extended time frame. The final potential factor to explain the outperformance of the shifted indexes is the change in the supply-demand balance for rolling contracts in the futures market. As the number of index investors increased, the cost of rolling futures at the front of the curve rose.

DIVERSIFICATION ACROSS COMMODITIES HELPS THE INTELLIGENT INDEX INVESTOR

From Exhibit 7-5, it seems that the return difference between the contracts in the DJUBSCI and those in the two-month shifted DJUBSCI presents a fantastic opportunity for the specialists, or "locals," in each of the underlying commodity markets that make up the DJUBSCI. However, the opportunity for locals in each commodity market to profit from the index activity is more risky than the exhibit would suggest. The exhibit overestimates the perceived opportunity because the return difference is an aggregation of the performance difference across the roughly 20 markets that make up the DJUBSCI. The relative performance of such a strategy on any one commodity within the index is often considerably more volatile. For example, the two-month shifted index only underperformed the regular DJUBSCI in 12% of the months from 2004 onward. However, in crude oil, the largest single commodity in the DJUBSCI, the WTI shifted index underperformed the WTI crude oil subindex one-third of the time. In other words, the probability of losing money during any one month doing the same type of bear-spread trade in just crude oil was nearly three times higher than doing it on the whole index. The reason for this is that such a trade in only one market is subject to unexpected changes in the fundamentals of that market. If crude oil inventories suddenly decline more than expected, the convenience yield will rise, and the front contracts will outperform. Similarly, event risk, such as a hurricane disrupting the supply of natural gas or a drought decreasing crop yields, dramatically increases the risk of such a trade in individual commodities. Therefore, a diversified basket, which spreads out the idiosyncratic risks found in each market, is generally the best way to capture the distortions introduced by the index. Since intelligent commodity index investors typically trade and possess knowledge about a broad range of markets, they are among some of the players most well suited for benefiting from these distortions.

Qualitatively, the return difference between the shifted commodity indexes and the standard commodity indexes was greatest from 2004 to mid–2006. Interestingly, 2004 was the beginning of widespread commodity index investing, and it was July 2006 when Dow Jones first started publishing shifted indexes. From mid-2006 onward, the return difference between shifted and regular commodity indexes has continued to decline. Whether this decline indicates a lowered risk premium in Keynes's normal backwardation framework or a reduced liquidity premium around the major indexes rolling from one contract to the next is difficult to say. However, the end result is the same. The calendar spreads at the front of the curve appear to contain lower levels of risk premium.

In 2010, the average monthly return difference between the shifted indexes and the regular DJUBSCI was back to the average pre-2004 level. Given the decline in return differences between shifted rolls and the regular indexes, it is increasingly important for sophisticated index investors to have strong risk management and knowledge of the evolving fundamentals of each major commodity market. In the past, the overall tailwind of positive shifted roll performance meant almost all broad-based baskets that held exposure out the curve would provide superior returns to the standard index. Going forward, if investors are to generate alpha from such spread strategies, they will be well served to develop an understanding about the current relative value of the convenience yield as well as a forward view on commodity-specific supply and demand fundamentals.

Indexes that broadly hold commodity exposure out the curve, either statically in a shifted index or through a dynamic approach like optimized roll yield, have gained increased popularity in recent years. For investors or managers placing growing risk in these types of strategies, it is very important to consider the beta of these deferred strategies against that of the more traditional front-month indexes, particularly when these deferred strategies are being implemented for the purposes of alpha. Investors allocating to deferred indexes to generate alpha can have a significant amount of implied beta if they substitute $1 million of notional of index with $1 million notional in a deferred index. Exhibit 7-6 shows the beta between the DJUBSCI and the DJUBSCI three-month shifted. Over the last few years, the average beta has been 0.95, but prior to this, the beta averaged 0.75. Even if the beta continues to average 0.95, this means that for every $100 of regular front-month DJUBSCI exposure that investors replace with a three-month shifted index, they gain only $95 of equivalent exposure. While the alpha generated in recent years from these strategies has been so large that any beta between deferred and front-month indexes has tended not to matter, going forward if commodity markets become more efficient and the risk premium between deferred contracts and front-month contracts is reduced, the management of this beta exposure will begin to be more important to an investor's risk-adjusted performance.

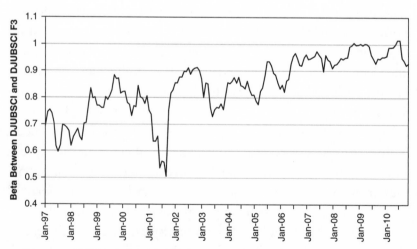

Exhibit 7-6 **Rolling 12-Month Beta Between the DJUBSCI and DJUBSCI Three-Month Forward**

Source: Bloomberg, PIMCO, as of December 31, 2010

SEASONAL STRATEGIES

Seasonal commodities tend to present many of the most lucrative opportunities in terms of calendar trading. The primary reason for this is that many seasonal commodities such as natural gas or wheat embed a significant risk premium in the price of particular contract months. This risk premium results in price differences between certain contract months of a given commodity that should not persist under most states of the world. However, the volatility or risk of these price differentials causes many investors to refrain from trading these forward spreads and harvesting the associated risk premiums. Index investors, with their steady capital base and long-term horizon, can look to structurally capture this premium by looking for attractive times to sell these spreads.

Seasonals in Natural Gas

A classic example of such a spread is the March–April spread in natural gas. This spread has been termed the *widow maker* by those who regularly trade natural gas. Given that this spread was one of the main positions that brought down hedge fund giant Amaranth, its name certainly appears to be justified. The reason this spread got its name is because it exhibits tremendous volatility. The reason the spread shows such large volatility has to do with the seasonality of demand for natural gas.

Natural gas inventories are built up from April through October and drawn down to accommodate larger heating demand during the winter months from November to March. Since demand exceeds supply during the winter, there need to be sufficient natural gas inventories to meet demand through March. If inventories are too low, prices would have to increase dramatically in order to reduce demand and ration the limited inventories that did remain. However, once March arrives and inventories are sufficient, storage operators have one of two choices, either sell the gas now or hold it until the following winter. Given inventories will be building from April through October, there

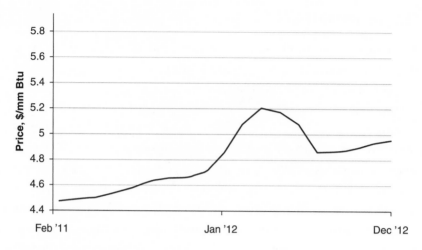

Exhibit 7-7 Natural Gas Forward Curve

Source: Bloomberg, as of January 25, 2011

will likely be substantial opportunities to rebuild stocks. Therefore, excess inventories that were serving as a buffer to the risk of running out of supply are sold, and the price of March tends to ultimately expire at a discount to April at the end of the winter. This phenomenon is what gives rise, in Exhibit 7-7, to the shape of the natural gas forward curve. In this snapshot of the forward curve the nearby March–April spread is trading in contango as inventories are comfortable for the current winter, however deferred March–April spreads continue to trade in a sizable backwardation.

Exhibit 7-8 shows the March–April natural gas spread for the past 17 years. We look at the spread on a percentage basis relative to the April contract to normalize for the fact that natural gas prices have varied from below $2 to above $10 over this period. We normalize by the April price, as this tends to be the more stable month; looking at the spread as a percentage of the March price results in under-stating the occasional violent moves upward when there is concern over an inventory shortage. The diamonds show where the spread started at the beginning of each April, and the squares show where the spread expired near the end of February of the following year.

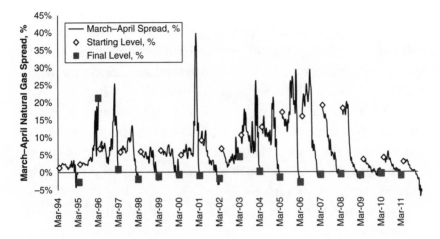

Exhibit 7-8   March–April Natural Gas Spread, as a Percentage of the April Price

Source: Bloomberg, PIMCO, as of January 31, 2011

Based upon the end-of-February levels, it would be impossible to think of this spread as a widow maker. In 16 of the last 17 years, the spread has settled within 5% of flat. In only one year did the spread expire more than 5% backwardated, and that was after the brutally cold winter of 1995.

The average ending level of the spread across all years has been just 1.5% backwardated. However, the average starting level of the spread has been 8.5% backwardated across all years. If this spread was purely a function of future inventory expectations, that would suggest that the market continually understimates the ending inventory level almost every year. But this seasonal relationship is driven just as much by future inventory expectations as it is by risk premium. The March–April natural gas spread is basically an option on running out of inventories, which would result in a dramatic price spike. Similar to options where there are more natural buyers than sellers, the same is true with winter natural gas. Power producers and others who need sufficient supplies are natural buyers of winter natural gas, but there are relatively few natural sellers. This presents an opportunity for index investors to be structural liquidity providers to the market, much as in the case of options (a topic we will explore in detail in the chapter on volatility strategies). Despite the regular expiry of the March–April natural gas spread near flat, as Exhibit 7-8 shows, the volatility of this spread is very high throughout the year owing to the risk of hurricanes disrupting supply and fears of cold winter. All these events can have huge impacts on the risk premium the market charges; and just like options, it is important to manage risk appropriately and have a model for assessing the value in underwriting such risk.

In addition to the March–April spread in natural gas pricing in a substantial risk premium, the other months in natural gas tend to display the same pattern of risk premium, just on a less pronounced scale. The concern about adequate supply in natural gas markets causes a regular risk premium to be built into the curve. The reason for this is that there is a common concern that due to a cold spell or hurricane or some other event, there will be insufficient supply available. However, as the front month approaches maturity and supply certainty becomes more and more probable, that risk premium slowly declines, resulting in the front-month contract underperforming more distant contracts. This phenomenon gives rise to a front contract that regularly fails to realize the forward prices. We can study this further by looking at the long-term performance of an index that rolls front month natural gas futures contracts on a monthly basis relative to an index that rolls natural gas in more deferred contracts.

Exhibit 7-9 shows the performance of four different natural gas indexes. The index labeled Jan-Jan Rolling rolls annually from the nearby January contract to the next January contract at the end of each September. Similarly, the index labeled Jul-Jul Rolling rolls annually from the nearby July contract to the next July contract at the end of each March. The other investable index included was the standard S&P GSCI natural gas subindex, which rolls natural gas each month from the first nearby contract month to

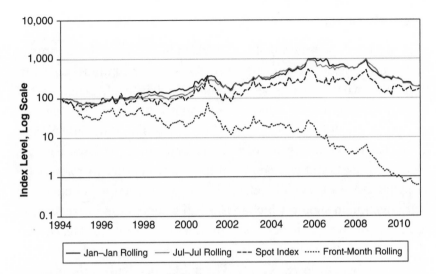

Exhibit 7-9   **A Comparison of the Performance of Four Different Natural Gas Indexes**

Source: Bloomberg, Standard & Poor's, PIMCO, as of December 31, 2010

the next nearby contract month. Finally, a spot natural gas price index, which is not investable, that shows the overall movement of spot natural gas prices was included for comparison purposes. The exhibit is in log scale to show the steady underperformance of the front-month rolling index versus both the spot index and the indexes that hold exposure further out the curve. This steady underperformance of the rolling front-month index is due to the constant risk premium embedded in the price of nearby natural gas contracts, as described above.

By showing indexes that hold both January and July contracts, we can conclude that the underperformance of the monthly rolling index is not a result of holding natural gas during a particular seasonal period and that the risk premium embedded in the futures curve is isolated at the front of the curve. Savvy index investors will often choose to hold some of their natural gas exposure out the curve to avoid paying this risk premium embedded in the market.

Seasonality in Corn

The same risk premium that is embedded in the front of the natural gas curve tends to be a feature seen across other commodities with large seasonal imbalances between supply and demand. A chart of the forward curve in corn is shown in Exhibit 7-10. Notice the regular pattern of prices rising from December to July. This is because North American corn is mostly harvested from September to November and then must be stored for the rest of the year to ensure that adequate supplies are available. Therefore, December is the futures contract with maximum supply, which makes it the contract most frequently used by growers to hedge their production. From the December contract, prices tend to increase to the July contract, which is the point of seasonally lowest supply. The market needs to set the price in July above the price in December to give commercial participants the necessary incentives to store corn throughout the year.

Just as in the case of natural gas, as we go through the year and ending stocks of corn become more certain, it often becomes apparent that there will be sufficient inventories to meet expected demand. As this conclusion becomes more and more certain, the risk

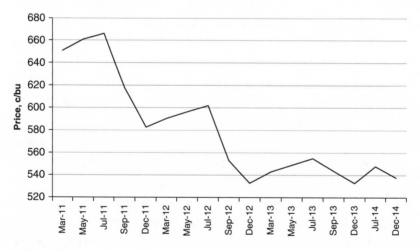

Exhibit 7-10 Corn Forward Curve

Source: Bloomberg, as of January 27, 2011

premium that is embedded in the market slowly declines, and the spread between the July contract and the December contract slowly shrinks and often ultimately shifts into contango. However, every so often the opposite is true, and the markets project inventories that are insufficient to meet demand. In these instances, prices can rise dramatically to try and reduce consumption or defer it until the next crop year when supply will likely be more plentiful. This is what happened in the 1995–1996 crop year in corn as well as in the 2010–2011 crop year. In both these crop years, the ratio of ending-year stocks to total use fell to below 6%.

A history of the spread between the July and December corn contracts is shown in Exhibit 7-11. On average, the starting level for the spread has been 11 cents, while the average ending level for the spread has been negative 4 cents. Assuming this difference is all from risk premium suggests the risk premium has averaged 15 cents over the past 15 years. However, from year to year, the risk premium has not been constant; some years the risk premium has been large, and other years it has been small. In particular, like other insurance

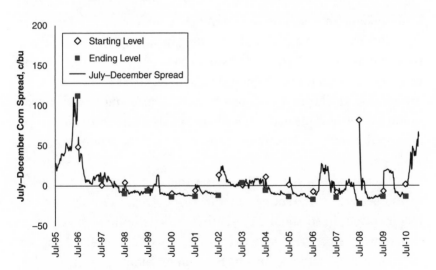

Exhibit 7-11 **Spread Between the July and December Corn Contracts, 1995–2010**

Source: Bloomberg, PIMCO, as of December 31, 2010

markets, the risk premium generally appears to be large following years of large price increases or high volatility. Such was clearly the case following the 1995–1996 crop year and also after the run-up in corn prices in late 2006.

While the March–April natural gas and July–December corn spreads were highlighted in this chapter, the same pattern of risk premium can be shown to exist across the futures curve of other markets with strong seasonal supply-demand imbalances. The risk premium in these markets is similar to the richness in the options market (a topic we will explore in detail in the chapter on volatility strategies). The risk premium is necessary to compensate investors and speculators for assuming the risk associated with the possibility that these spreads could move dramatically higher.

Given the index investors' natural long position across multiple commodity markets, these investors are in a unique position to capture this risk premium. In an effort to capture this risk premium, index investors can move contracts out the curve by selling the nearby contract and buying a more deferred contract. This means that the investors will likely underperform during a short-term spike up in prices or an extreme inventory shortfall; but since index investors typically hold positions in multiple commodities, they can achieve substantial diversification benefits. The inventory dynamics and fundamentals in the natural gas market are very different from those of the corn market. Capturing this risk premium across multiple markets with uncorrelated inventory and supply and demand fundamentals helps to reduce the size of potential underperformance.

In addition to the risk premium that is reflected in the price spread between different contract months, there are other signs of risk premium in seasonal commodity markets. Exhibit 7-12 shows the average percent return in corn over the past 20 years. As you can see, the average returns during the summer months are noticeably worse than the rest of the year. The summer months represent the period of lowest inventories right before the harvest, which occurs predominantly from September to November. In other words, the

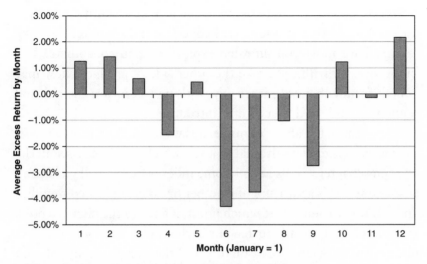

Exhibit 7-12 **Average Excess Return by Month, 1990–2009**

Source: Bloomberg, Standard & Poor's, as of December 31, 2009

greatest risk of a dramatic price spike is during the summer months; and indeed this has been the case historically, with the majority of very large moves in the price of corn occurring during the summer. Since corn prices have a fat tail risk skewed to the upside during the summer months, the fact that there is a tendency for prices to decline on average fits very well with the risk premium argument and the trading pattern discussed previously in corn spreads. The market pays investors willing to bear the risk associated with low inventory levels or a worse-than-expected harvest. Similar patterns of price performance during periods of seasonally high risk can be seen across other commodities with large seasonal swings in supply and demand.

The seasonality of corn prices is also related to producer hedging practices. In addition to embedded risk premium leading to negative returns during the summer months, this is also the time when a significant portion of producer hedging is completed. Being aware of the seasonality of producer flows across markets can be very helpful for commodity index investors. After all, and as mentioned previously, one of the natural roles of commodity index participants is to serve as a source of liquidity to the producer community. Producers tend to be the dominant hedgers in most markets, as they tend to have more concentrated exposures than consumers. The index investor willing to take the other side of producer flow may benefit from enhanced returns by working to capture the risk and liquidity premium that such flow introduces.

In light of the above example, it is worthwhile to briefly revisit the idea of optimized roll yield indexes, which were discussed in the previous chapter. As discussed, some indexes look at roll yield in an absolute sense as a measure of whether or not to hold a commodity and as a way to determine which point, if any, on the curve to hold. If commodities are all treated similarly as one homogenous asset class, without regard to seasonality and the specific nature of each commodity market, the results are often highly suboptimal. The case previously discussed in corn is a classic example. Since inventories are lowest during the summer months, the risk premium tends to be highest. This is associated with a high convenience yield and a low roll yield. The DJUBSCI and S&P GSCI corn subindex rolls five times a year, in February, April, June, August, and November. The historic roll yield realized by the index for those five roll periods is shown in Exhibit 7-13. As expected, the roll yield is the highest when inventories are low, and the lowest roll yield is seen in November just after the corn harvest. The optimized roll yield strategy, which seeks to maximize roll yield, would be most likely to hold corn during June and July, the points of lowest inventory. Interestingly though, the best roll yield, during the June roll, is also the period with the worst average return (Exhibit 7-12). This is why it is so important to understand and account for the existence of risk premium and other fundamental differences when using one set of rules like optimized roll yield across multiple commodities.

Calendar spreads in commodities tell investors a great deal about the market's forward-looking expectations for inventories and the supply-demand balance. In addition, calendar spreads are a source of potential alpha for commodity index investors that can

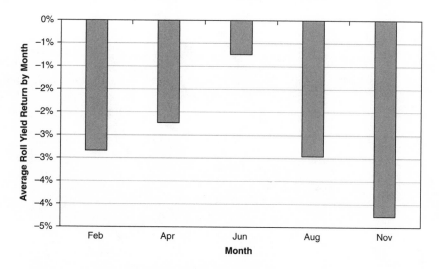

Exhibit 7-13 **Average Roll Yield Return by Month**

Source: Bloomberg, Standard & Poor's, as of December 31, 2009

disentangle the relation between the market's forward inventory expectations and the risk or liquidity premium embedded in the calendar spreads. As we have shown, these premiums often arise from consumer or producer hedging or large seasonal mismatches between supply and demand. The key is to use fundamental analysis regarding inventory levels, future supply and demand, and storage costs in order to decompose forward calendar spreads into a market expectations component and a risk premium component. This will help investors to assess whether or not they are being appropriately compensated for selling such risk premium, and this analysis can also uncover instances where tail risk hedges might be purchased cheaply.

The calendar or seasonal strategies discussed in this chapter provide the astute investor a rich source of potential outperformance by taking exposure in the same commodity at different points on the futures curve. In the next chapter on substitution strategies, we discuss another means of pursuing outperformance: making a choice between closely related but different commodities.

CHAPTER 8

Substitution

Major indexes such as the DJUBSCI and S&P GSCI are designed to provide investors both liquid and diversified exposure to the commodities markets. Therefore, it is by design that the major commodity indexes screen prospective commodity contracts based upon liquidity. The DJUBSCI and S&P GSCI consist primarily of the most liquid markets for each of the major commodities traded around the world. However, in addition to the contracts referenced by these commodity indexes, there are often similar, closely related commodities that trade on different exchanges around the world. Investors can often earn incremental returns by moving from the benchmark contracts used in constructing an index to closely related alternatives that provide very similar economic exposures.

For example, the DJUBSCI references the WTI crude oil contract that trades on the New York Mercantile Exchange. Alternatives to the WTI crude oil contract are the Brent crude oil contract that trades on the Intercontinental Exchange and the Oman crude oil contract that trades on the Dubai Mercantile Exchange. In addition, moving away from the major exchanges, various other grades of crude oil are traded globally on an OTC basis.

As another example, the DJUBSCI references the wheat contract traded on the Chicago Board of Trade (CBOT), but there are other wheat contracts that trade on the Kansas City Board of Trade (KCBT), the Minneapolis Grain Exchange (MGE), the Euronext exchange in Paris, the Australian Stock Exchange, etc. Not only do these different contracts represent the price of crude oil or wheat in different locations, but they also have different quality specifications, delivery mechanisms, market participants, liquidity, and order flow.

Understanding the liquidity, supply and demand fundamentals, and pricing differences among all these related markets allows a commodity index investor to substitute very similar commodities for one another in an effort to enhance the returns of a naive broad basket of commodities, where weights and contracts are determined by little more than liquidity or total global production. As we will illustrate, substitution strategies can be either tactical or structural, arising from short-term dislocations in the pricing of two similar commodities or from a systematic return advantage that often accrues to long-term holders of one commodity over the other.

Substitution strategies can often be thought of as harvesting a liquidity premium. Many market participants value liquidity and are willing to pay for it. A long-term, well-capitalized commodity index investor may be able to earn an excess return by substituting a more liquid commodity with a less liquid but largely similar commodity. One can think of analogies in equity or fixed-income investing where large-cap stocks are likely to command a liquidity premium over small-cap stocks in essentially the same industry, or where on-the-run Treasuries command a liquidity premium over off-the-run Treasuries even though both are liabilities of the U.S. government and often only a few months apart in maturity. A long-term investor would often be willing to give up some liquidity in order to earn the higher yield offered by off-the-run Treasuries. In commodities, understanding the cause of the price discrepancy between two similar commodities, and the risks involved in purchasing one over the other, forms the core of any substitution-based outperformance strategy.

WHEAT AS AN EXAMPLE

The easiest way to understand the decision process and possibilities involved with trading substitutable commodities is through an example. Wheat is an excellent place to start for three reasons. First, there are many global wheat contracts available to investors. Second, in the long run there is a well-defined price relationship among the various grades of wheat, but in the short term each contract has very different liquidity and fundamental factors. These short-term factors can cause the relative price between different grades of wheat to diverge from longer run relationships and provide excellent relative value trading opportunities. Finally, and most important, the wheat market offers a very clear example of both structural and tactical substitution opportunities. While the number of tactical substitution-type trading opportunities is almost unlimited, the number of structural opportunities is considerably more sparse.

The most liquid wheat contract in the world is the soft red winter wheat (SRW) contract traded on the CBOT. SRW is a class of wheat with relatively low protein, and it is grown primarily in states just east of the Mississippi River and along the lower half of the eastern seaboard. SRW is predominantly used for cakes and pastries.

Another wheat contract that is similar and highly correlated with the SRW contract is the hard red winter wheat (HRW) contract traded on the KCBT. HRW is a higher-protein class of wheat used for breads and hard rolls. It is grown across the Great Plains in states such as Kansas and Oklahoma, and it is the predominant type of wheat grown in the United States. All else equal, the additional protein content of HRW means that it trades at a premium to the lower-protein SRW.

In 2010, the average daily volume of the CBOT's SRW contract was around 90,000 contracts, compared with only 20,000 for the KCBT's HRW contract. The SRW contract's superior liquidity results in it being the dominant source of wheat exposure for commodity indexes such as the DJUBSCI and S&P GSCI, despite the fact that the size of the HRW crop is much larger than the SRW crop. In addition, when macro hedge funds or other large speculative players seek to place large bets on changes in the price of wheat, they typically use the SRW contract because of its liquidity.

A chart of the price difference between the HRW and SRW contracts is shown in Exhibit 8-1. Notice that the price of HRW almost always trades at a premium to SRW. On average, from 2000 to 2010, HRW traded at a 25-cent premium to SRW; however, that is by no means a stable level, as HRW traded anywhere from a how-many cent discount to 100 cents over SRW. It is the volatility of this spread that creates substitution opportunities for the intelligent index investor.

The spread in price between the HRW and SRW contracts should in theory only respond to the differences in fundamentals between these two classes of wheat. For example, are the inventories of SRW more or less plentiful than those of HRW? What is the relative strength of export and domestic demand for each class of wheat? How does the protein content of SRW and HRW compare this year relative to average? Answering these types of questions

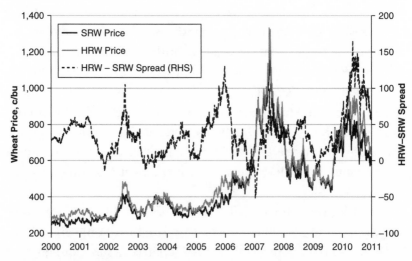

Exhibit 8-1   **Price Difference Between the HRW and SRW Contracts**

Source: Bloomberg, as of October 31, 2011

about fundamentals and supply and demand can lead to an estimate of fair value for the spread between the SRW and HRW contracts. In practice, that fair value estimate does not always correspond to where the spread is actually trading, resulting in opportunities for index investors to enhance results while simultaneously providing liquidity to the markets.

Let's consider the summer of 2010 as an example. In June, HRW was trading at a 30-cent premium to SRW. The global wheat market appeared amply supplied, and according to the CFTC Commitments of Traders report, speculative positioning was, on the whole, very short wheat. SRW prices traded as low as $4.28, the lowest level in over three years. Then the balance in the market changed rapidly as news of a drought across Russia and parts of Europe caused wheat prices to rally. The global supply of wheat was suddenly less plentiful than had been expected. The rally in wheat was exacerbated by substantial short covering from hedge funds and other speculative players that held short positions prior to the Russian news. Most of these short positions were on the more liquid SRW contract, and so as wheat prices continued to rally and there was more and more short covering, the price of SRW rose more than the price of HRW.

Looking at just the fundamentals of the wheat markets, HRW should have outperformed SRW. The Russian spring wheat crop has a larger share of higher-protein milling wheat, and reduced Russian production typically means increased export demand from the United States for HRW. Therefore, this should ultimately be bullish for the spread between HRW and SRW prices. However, in the short run, the relative positioning in these two markets can be a bigger driver of prices than the fundamentals. In this case, the speculative community was very short the SRW contract, and so the SRW contract outperformed as speculators covered their shorts and other speculators established long positions. As wheat prices climbed higher and higher, CTAs and other trend followers sought to get long wheat, a view predominantly expressed through the more liquid

Chicago contract. These factors caused the SRW contract and the HRW contract to trade at the same price, while fundamentals suggested that hard red wheat should trade at a substantial premium to soft red wheat. Over the course of the next four months, the fundamentals were ultimately born out as the HRW contract traded out to a 70-cent (10%) premium to the SRW contract. This series of events is the perfect opportunity for intelligent index investors. Index investors are typically long-term, well-capitalized market participants; so they are able to provide liquidity to the market, in this case by selling the SRW contract and buying the HRW contract with the expectation that, over time, fundamentals will reassert themselves and the spread between the contracts will go back to levels dictated by fundamentals, not positioning.

Timing is critical in tactically taking advantage of short-term distortions between substitutable commodity markets. When distortions such as the one described in wheat occur, there is often some fundamental catalyst that will initiate the return to fair value. In the case of wheat that was just described, it was the start of the U.S. export season and the accompanying strong demand for hard red wheat exports, given their attractive pricing versus that for soft red wheat. In addition to a catalyst for a return to fair value, many relationships have points of high resistance that are difficult to overcome. Understanding where these points exist can provide valuable information about the best time to enter a spread in order to limit downside risk. For example, in the case of wheat, HRW can be delivered against the CBOT SRW contract. This doesn't happen often, given that HRW is a higher-quality wheat; however, it is possible. Theoretically, if the spread got too wide, then it would be possible to go long the KCBT HRW contract, take delivery of the wheat, ship it to a delivery location for the SRW contract, and deliver this position against a short in the SRW contract. The cost of shipping wheat from an HRW contract delivery location in Kansas to an SRW contract delivery location in Illinois is roughly 20 cents. Therefore, the 20-cent level is a critical point where the spread between the price of the HRW and SRW contracts tends to show strong resistance.

LONG-TERM FACTORS IN WHEAT

In addition to the tactical trading of the price spread between hard and soft wheat, which involves profiting through fundamental moves of this spread, a second, more permanent and powerful factor is at play. Historically, there has been a persistent, structurally based roll yield difference between the KCBT HRW and the CBOT SRW contracts. Part of this roll yield difference comes from the fact that the storage cost, which is mandated by the exchange, has historically been lower on the HRW contract, on the order of 1–2% from 2000 to 2009. (In 2010, the CME changed the fixed storage rate for the SRW contract to a variable storage rate. This change has seen the storage cost of SRW increase threefold and go from the historic 1–2% above HRW to as much as 20% above HRW.)

The difference in roll yield is also driven by a difference in the makeup of market participants. The physical crop of SRW in the U.S. is significantly smaller than the HRW crop. Given that the size of the HRW futures market is smaller while the crop is larger, the HRW contract tends to structurally have a greater percentage of commercial participation from producers and elevators that are generally seeking to hedge physical inventory, while the SRW contract tends to structurally have a greater amount of long exposure from speculative and index-oriented participants. The typically greater demand for short commercial interest in the HRW contract results in a greater demand for the short rolling of contracts, i.e., buying nearby and selling deferred contracts. To result in a balanced market, speculative accounts must take the other side of this trade, and the roll from one contract to the next tends to trade at a lesser contango than it otherwise would. Similarly, the SRW contract sees the opposite flow, with speculators and index investors demanding liquidity to roll their long positions. Therefore, to balance flow in each market, the SRW contract should trade at a greater contango and closer to full carry than the HRW contract.

Historically this roll yield difference can be easily seen by looking at the chart in Exhibit 8-2, which shows the average annualized roll

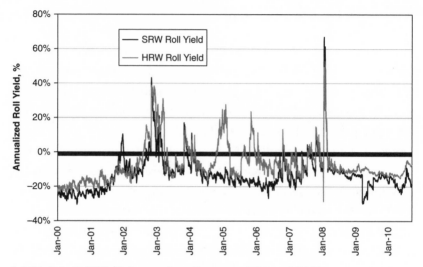

Exhibit 8-2 Roll Yield Comparison Between SRW and HRW

Source: Bloomberg, PIMCO, as of December 31, 2010

yield between the front two contracts for both the HRW and SRW contracts. From 2000 to 2010, the average roll yield for the HRW contract has been −7%, compared with −13% for SRW. Therefore, an index investor would have earned an average positive carry of 6% per year by being long HRW and short SRW. Since the addition of the variable storage rate in the SRW contract, the roll yield divergence between the two markets has become even more extreme, reaching as wide as 15–20% in the latter half of 2010.

The fact that substitution between the SRW and HRW contracts has significant return potential from both the tactical and structural perspective is what makes it so attractive. The tactical returns come about from spread movements between the prices of these two contracts. As discussed previously, the spread often shows divergence from a fundamental "fair" value due to liquidity and positioning differences between the two contracts. The structural returns arise from different storage rates, levels of liquidity, and market participants. These market differences typically manifest themselves in a continued roll yield differential between these two contracts. Understanding these structural market differences in combination with the fundamentals of each market is the key to creating profitable substitution trades for the intelligent index investor.

Index investors have a natural advantage over many other speculative investors in capturing these types of structural substitution trades in the commodity markets both because they start with a natural long exposure across many markets and because they have a long-term orientation. For example, since index investors tend to hold a diversified basket of commodities, they typically will have a long exposure to the wheat market. They can decide to hold their long wheat exposure in any market they chose by reducing exposure in the index-specified contract and increasing exposure in another wheat contract. The index investor's gross notional exposure doesn't change.

By contrast, if speculators seek to take advantage of the spread differential between these two markets, they have to put on a long and a short trade in each market. They now have twice the gross notional exposure of those index investors who just replaced some of their long exposure. Since most spread trades involve contracts on different exchanges, speculators are required to post margins on the total gross notional even though it is a spread trade that generally involves substantially less risk than an outright exposure on either market. This means the speculators must post twice as much margin as the index investors, meaning that the speculators' return on capital at risk will be half as large. Substitution trades by their nature tend to have relatively low volatility and, hence, low returns per unit of notional. Such a trade would often only be attractive to speculators if they could significantly lever their position. Since speculators are often levered while most index investors are fully collateralized, index investors tend to have much greater holding power and can typically ride out adverse price movements. This gives index investors an advantage, as they can avoid getting stopped out of a spread position at exactly the wrong time.

Energy	Brent vs. WTI Crude Oil
	Gasoil vs. Heating Oil
	U.S. vs. U.K. Natural Gas
Base Metals	LME vs. COMEX Copper
Grains	Euronext vs. MGE Wheat
	Tokyo Grain Exchange vs. CME Corn
Other Agricultural	Arabica vs. Robusta Coffee
	Euronext vs. ICE Cocoa

Exhibit 8-3 **Examples of Common Substitution Trades Between Different Grades or Locations of the Same Commodity**

Source: PIMCO

The spread between the price of SRW and HRW contracts is just one example of a spread opportunity between different grades of the same commodity or the same commodity at different locations. Exhibit 8-3 lists a few further examples of common substitution trades between different grades or locations of the same commodity. Each of the markets highlighted in the exhibit offers index investors tactical opportunities to take a view on changes in the relative price of each commodity based upon fundamental factors.

SUBSTITUTION IN CRUDE OIL

For an example of substitution in the energy space, consider the difference between WTI and Brent crude oil. They are both considered light, sweet crude oils, although WTI is slightly lighter and sweeter. Being lighter and sweeter, WTI is easier to refine and has historically tended to trade at a premium to Brent. Besides quality, these two grades of crude also have a location differential. WTI crude oil's delivery location is Cushing, Oklahoma. Brent is a representation of the price of crude oil in the North Sea. This means that WTI crude oil tends to be relatively less globally mobile, and pricing must reflect relative supply and demand in and around the Midwestern United States. By contrast, Brent is a waterborne crude oil that can easily be shipped anywhere globally.

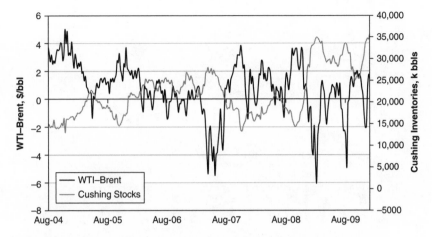

Exhibit 8-4 **WTI—Brent Price Spread and Oil Inventories at Cushing, Oklahoma**

Source: Bloomberg, DOE, as of December 31, 2009

The overall supply-demand balance in the Midwest can be approximated by looking at the level of inventories in Cushing. When demand is strong and exceeding available supply, oil inventories serve as the buffer to balance supply and demand. As inventories decline, the relative premium of WTI should rise in order to increase oil imports and ration the remaining inventory levels. Similarly, when demand is insufficient to absorb all supply, the excess oil must flow into storage. To lower incremental supply, the price of WTI should fall relative to Brent, which is a global crude benchmark, thereby discouraging imports into the U.S. crude market.

The above example of the spread between WTI and Brent focused on the dynamic driving prices for the front-month and shorter-dated futures contract. At the front of the curve, it is physical supply and demand that typically dictates pricing; and for an index investor to tactically profit from the spread between WTI and Brent requires having an accurate view on future supply-demand balances in the Midwestern United States, which will ultimately be reflected in inventory levels at Cushing. But even if the index investor doesn't have a strong view of inventories in Cushing over the

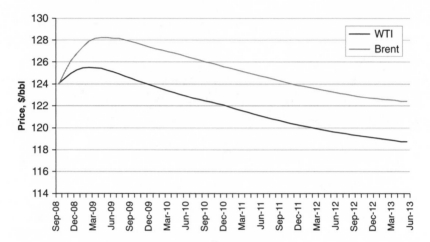

Exhibit 8-5 **WTI and Brent Crude Oil Futures Curve**

Source: Bloomberg, as of July 31, 2008

next few months, there are still market dislocations that can be taken advantage of. For example, Exhibit 8-5 shows the spread between the futures curve for WTI and Brent crude oil at the end of July 2008, just weeks after the peak in crude oil prices. At the front of the curve, WTI and Brent were trading at parity with one another, a price that could ultimately be rich or cheap, depending on the future direction of Cushing inventories. However, the longer-dated contracts appear grossly mispriced, with the price of WTI trading at a $3.5 discount to the price of Brent two years out.

Looking at the history of the spread between WTI and Brent in the 10 years leading up to 2008, WTI very rarely traded at more than a $3 discount to Brent. Given this large divergence, was the market really forecasting that inventories at Cushing were going to become much higher over the next two years and then remain high indefinitely? In reality, the spread got to such wide levels because of an imbalance between supply and demand and a lack of liquidity in longer dated crude oil futures. It turns out that WTI is a much more common contract to reference for producer hedging deals, and there was a substantial amount of selling in the long end of the WTI curve when prices in oil were near all-time highs.

In addition, refiners in Europe generally participate in more hedging than U.S. refineries. As spreads between oil products—namely, diesel and heating oil—and oil were still at very wide levels, refiners in Europe sought to hedge future production by buying long-dated Brent crude and selling forward crude products. This flow of producers selling WTI and refiners buying Brent drove longer-dated crude spreads to fundamentally unjustified levels.

Such extreme opportunities out the curve are often the most common sources of substitution opportunities in the commodity complex. The reason for this is that while supply and demand often keeps nearby contract prices adhering to tight, fundamentally grounded relationships, the longer-dated contracts are much more vulnerable to flow pressures, given their reduced liquidity. Such noneconomically justified spreads at the longer portion of commodity curves are an excellent opportunity for index investors to provide liquidity to the market and potentially earn a profit in doing so.

LONG-TERM FACTORS IN CRUDE OIL

Just as in the case of HRW and SRW, the best substitution trades for index investors tend to be those that have structural, persistent factors in addition to occasional short-term dislocations. In the case of WTI and Brent, there are structural factors to consider, some of which are more credible than others. The popular media has occasionally run stories about the very large contango in the front of the WTI crude oil curve. During these instances, the WTI curve was said to be in "super contango," and there were claims that "WTI is a broken benchmark." The explanation given for the behavior of the WTI market was frequently attributed to index investment or speculative activity, but this part of the claim seems very misdirected. Exhibit 8-6 shows the roll yield in WTI crude oil and the crude oil inventories in the Midwest (labeled "PADD 2" by the Department of Energy). Notice that the changes in the level of inventories explains a large portion of the changes in the roll yield, and when the roll yield gets very wide, i.e., in super contango, it is because

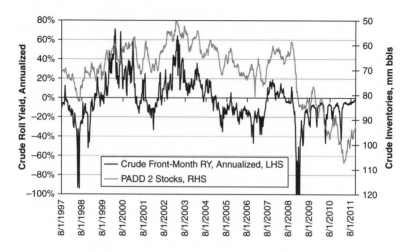

Exhibit 8-6   Roll Yield of Front Month Crude Oil Futures and Inventory Levels

Source: Bloomberg, DOE, PIMCO, as of August 31, 2011

inventories are very high. However, despite these claims about WTI being a broken contract due to investor activity being exaggerated, there are some structural factors that could result in WTI being structurally disadvantaged over the next few years.

Currently there are two structural long-term trends playing out in crude oil production in North America. The first is the increased growth of oil imports into the United States from Canada, due in part to growth in oil sands. The second trend is the explosive growth in U.S. Midwestern crude oil production, particularly from shale oil opportunities in states such as North Dakota. Exhibit 8-7 shows the production of crude oil from North Dakota from 1990 through the end of 2011. Due to the constraints on pipeline infrastructure, much of this crude finds its way into the Midwest, but it is unable to be transported out of the Midwest to the Gulf Coast. This means that Cushing, the delivery point for WTI, is likely to be generally better supplied than most crude oil markets globally. Going forward, this could keep the price of WTI at a sustained price discount to Brent and also cause roll yields in WTI to be lower than those in Brent on average.

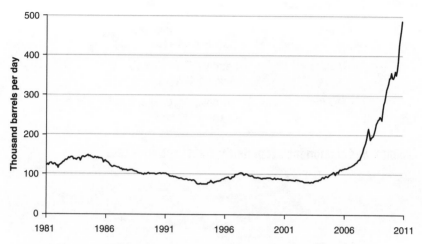

Exhibit 8-7   Monthly North Dakota Field Production of Crude Oil

Source: DOE, U.S. Energy Information Administration, as of December 31, 2011

INTERCOMMODITY SUBSTITUTION

The same principles discussed for intracommodity substitution also apply to intercommodity substitutions, such as wheat versus corn or crude oil versus natural gas. These commodities are still related but not as directly as the examples we studied above that involved different grades and geographic locations for the same commodity. For example, corn and wheat are related in the sense that a big run-up in wheat prices relative to corn would tend to result in more wheat and less corn planting in the following year. Similarly if the prices differed by a large amount, oil or coal-fired energy production could be replaced by natural gas. The big difference when looking at intercommodity substitutions is that the volatility increases and the definition of "fair" value often becomes more subjective. There is typically a relation between either the supply or demand but often no direct link. As such, price deviations frequently go to much greater extremes and can last much longer in intercommodity substitutions. The potential upside to intercommodity substitutions is that the set of available opportunities tends to be broader and more liquid than for intracommodity substitutions. Exhibit 8-8 presents a partial list of common intercommodity substitution trades.

Energy	Coal vs. Natural Gas
	Gasoline vs. Heating Oil
Metals	Lead vs. Zinc
	Gold vs. Silver
Grains	Corn vs. Soybeans
	Corn vs. Wheat

Exhibit 8-8 Common Intercommodity Substitution Trades

Source: PIMCO

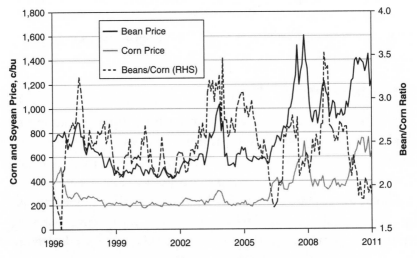

Exhibit 8-9 Price of Corn and Soybeans and the Soybean/Corn Ratio

Source: Bloomberg, as of September 30, 2011

Exhibit 8-9 shows the historic prices of soybeans and corn as well as the ratio between them. The long-run average ratio of the price of soybeans to the price of corn is 2.5, but it has ranged from 1.5 to 3.5. While corn and soybeans serve two different markets on the demand side, there is the potential for substitution on the supply side. Farmers in certain geographic regions can choose which of these two commodities to plant in order to maximize their expected profits. When the corn market is tighter than the soybean market, then more corn needs to be planted, and the market uses the relative prices between these commodities to send that signal to the farmer.

The index investor can use this long-run relationship, along with current fundamentals, in assessing the value of moving from one commodity to another. However, when the spread gets to extreme levels, it isn't clear that the observable fundamentals provide much information. The observable fundamentals often serve to justify the spread at its extreme levels; otherwise how would the spread have gotten so far out of line in the first place?

Exhibit 8-10 shows the ratio of soybeans to corn as well as the historical performance of a long position in corn and a short position in soybeans over the next one year. Notice that the current soybean/corn ratio is a very strong indicator of the future relative performance difference between those two commodities. Given this, it seems the market ends up too often falling victim to the common rationalization, "This time is different." While fundamentals certainly matter, having a long-term perspective on the structural link between such commodities can help index investors to understand

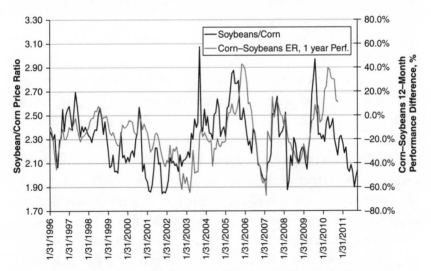

Exhibit 8-10 Soybeans to Corn Ratio and Future 12-Month Performance Difference of Corn–Soybeans

Source: Bloomberg, Standard & Poor's, as of September 30, 2011

what represents a good "value." In addition to the tactical trading opportunities described above between soybeans and corn, recall that there is also a structural difference between corn and soybeans from their different percentage storage rates. As in the prior substitution strategies we discussed, such a structural difference combined with a sense for tactical value is the key behind fully exploiting commodity substitution opportunities.

Substitution strategies need not involve commodities with a listed futures exchange. Looking at non-exchange-traded commodities allows index investors a very large, albeit often illiquid, set of opportunities. Some of the more regularly traded OTC markets include different grades of crude oil such as Louisiana Light Sweet as well as coal, freight, and iorn ore rhodium. At a minimum, monitoring such markets allows investors to assess whether or not there are any meaningful distortions from financial flows in the price of exchange-traded markets versus the more physically based OTC markets.

As shown in the case of the ratio between soybean and corn prices, looking at the relative prices of different commodities is a valuable tool in assessing value. In the case of corn and soybeans, that value is often realized in a relatively short time, on the order of months, as yearly planting cycles of both hemispheres tend to pull the ratio back to fair value. In the case of other commodities such as energy, the price divergences can persist for significantly longer. Exhibit 8-11 shows the price of oil, natural gas, and coal all converted to $/million Btu terms. The relative value among these commodities isn't typically realigned in months, as it is in corn and soybeans, but rather over many years. Relative switching between these different commodities can occur quickly only in a very marginal way. The main source of near-term substitution is found in power plants that can switch from coal to natural gas or vice versa, but the short-term switching capacity in the entire United States in 2011 was on the order of a few Bcf/day, whereas total daily consumption was nearly 70 Bcf/day. Industrial companies can work to use more natural gas feedstocks instead of oil-based feedstocks,

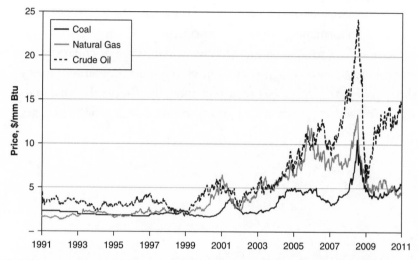

Exhibit 8-11   Crude Oil, Natural Gas, and Coal Prices on a $/mm Btu basis

Source: Bloomberg, PIMCO, as of December 31, 2010

but these types of changes generally involve significant research and have very long lead times.

The biggest area where oil could be displaced is in transportation. Gasoline consumption in the United States in 2010 was over 9 million barrels/day, or roughly 45% of U.S. oil demand. Given the growth in electric car technology, it seems that natural gas and coal (via power plants) may soon be competing with oil. Such a shift will take time, but it highlights the long-term upward pull that could be in place in coal and natural gas, given they are such cheap substitutes for crude oil.

In analyzing substitution opportunities, the best results are often obtained when investors consider not only the spot returns from expected price movements, but also the roll yield returns that may arise from structural differences between two commodities. As shown with examples in wheat and oil, structural return differences are often the result of storage pricing differences as well as different market participants, liquidity, supply-demand balances, and inventory levels. Ultimately, the best risk-adjusted return potential is available to index investors who can combine tactical trading opportunities with longer-term structural tailwinds.

So far, we have discussed three of the four broad classes of structural outperformance strategies—optimizing the carry or roll yield, exploiting seasonal distortions and risk premiums in calendar spreads, and finally substituting cheaper, but closely related, commodities to those held in the index. In the next chapter, we discuss the final major structural source of potential outperformance—volatility strategies.

CHAPTER 9

Volatility

The essence of intelligent commodity index investing consists of working to enhance the returns from holding a basket of commodity futures by capturing risk premium embedded in the various commodity markets. The options markets represent another rich source of risk premium that can be used to enhance the return potential of a commodity index investment. Fixed-income and equity investors may already be aware of yield enhancement strategies that involve selling options; similar strategies can be utilized in the commodity markets. In this chapter, we introduce the participants in the commodity options markets and the reasons for the existence of risk premiums. We point out certain differences between the commodities' option markets and the option markets in fixed-income and equities, and we show historical performances of different approaches to selling options or volatility in the commodity markets. Finally, we discuss some of the risks associated with such strategies.

OPTIONS AS AN INSURANCE POLICY

To understand why options represent a rich source of potential return for the commodity index investor, it is best to start by thinking about the major participants who trade commodity options. Call options are a means of guaranteeing the right to buy a commodity at a given price, and so they are often used by consumers of various commodities. For example, airlines and trucking companies buy call options on oil or oil products such as jet fuel and diesel to hedge their future demand. Given a crude oil price of $88/barrel for spot delivery and $90 for delivery in a year's time, an airline company may purchase call options on 1,000 contracts of crude oil with a strike of $95. This would give the airline the right to purchase 1 million barrels of crude oil for no greater than $95/barrel. This option purchase would cap the airline's cost in the case that crude oil prices rise from current levels, while still providing the flexibility to buy at lower prices should crude oil prices decline.

Put options are a means of guaranteeing the ability to sell a commodity at a given price. As such, producers of crude oil and natural gas will often buy puts to hedge some of their future production, and farmers will buy put options on corn or other agricultural commodities to guarantee a minimum price for their crop. Given spot crude oil prices at $88, crude oil producers could buy put options that give them the right to sell crude oil above, say, $70/barrel throughout the following year. This would guarantee them a selling price that is still comfortably above their marginal cost of production if prices were to fall. Across the commodity universe, there is a constant demand from producers to guarantee a minimum price for their production and from consumers to ensure a ceiling on their input costs.

A third group of commodity option buyers, in addition to producers and consumers, are investors in principal-protected structured notes. These are investors who want exposure to the upside in commodity prices, but not to the downside. Principal-protected notes became popular in recent years as a way for retail investors to participate in the rapid rise in commodity prices. A typical principal-protected note guarantees that investors will receive their principal back plus some upside participation in the returns from the underlying basket of commodities that the note references. Essentially, a principal-protected note is a long position in a basket of commodities plus an at-the-money put option. Therefore, investors buying such notes are implicitly purchasing put options on commodity indexes in order to protect against the possibility of a sell-off in commodity prices, resulting in option demand across all the commodities in the underlying index.

All the previous examples of option users in commodity markets were of buyers. This is because the natural users of options are hedgers who are essentially purchasing a type of "insurance" in an effort to guarantee a certain level of profitability in the case of adverse price movements. Just as in everyday life, natural buyers of insurance outnumber natural sellers, causing a structural supply imbalance such that the sellers of insurance require compensation for restoring equilibrium to the market. The same applies in the commodity options markets. There are many examples of natural option or insurance buyers, but few natural option or insurance sellers exist in amounts that can fill the needs of the buyers.

As long-term, unlevered participants in the commodity markets, commodity index investors are in a unique position to be sellers of options to the commodity producers and consumers in the market. Similar to insurance companies, commodity index investors are typically well capitalized (fully funded or unlevered) and have the ability to weather the occasional short-term drawdowns that occur even in long-term profitable insurance or option selling strategies. As with any insurance or option selling strategy, long-term viability is predicated on the appropriate sizing and risk management of positions, an issue we will address later in this chapter and also in the chapter on risk management.

The risk premium, often referred to as *richness*, embedded in commodity option prices is reflected in the implied volatility of the option. Implied volatility is the level of volatility that is required to make the model price—determined by an option pricing model such as Black-Scholes—equal to the actual market price of the option. In December 2010, the implied volatility for one-month at-the-money options on WTI crude oil was 30%. Using the $88/barrel price referenced earlier, this means that an option buyer would be betting

that on average the daily price move will be above $1.66.* Given
the premise that options are a form of insurance and should trade
rich, then implied volatility should structurally trade above realized
volatility, and this is in fact what we observe. For the month after
December 2010, the WTI crude oil price experienced an average
price volatility of just $1.28 per day, or a realized volatility of 23%.
Exhibit 9-1 shows the longer-term history of the level of implied
volatility for at-the-money options with one month to expiry on the
WTI crude oil contract and the subsequent realized volatility over
the following month. Over the period from mid–2007 to the end of
2010, the level of implied volatility was an average of 4 percentage
points higher than the level of realized volatility. It turns out that
even during a period of time that included the turbulent financial
crisis of 2008, option buyers on average still paid a premium above
realized volatility for their exposure.

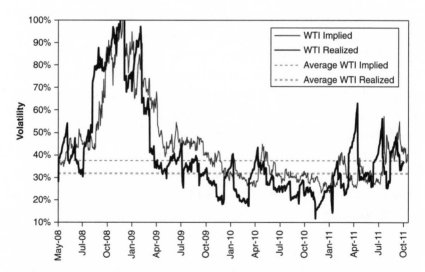

Exhibit 9-1 **WTI Crude—Implied and Realized Volatility**

Source: Bloomberg

* The daily move is calculated by taking the annualized volatility and scaling it
to a daily volatility, then multiplying by the price. For example, 30%/sqrt(252) *
88 = $1.66.

Commodity index investors have a number of different opportunities to sell options and capture the option risk premium. However, each strategy carries unique risks that should be carefully
analyzed and compared. For example, should investors sell shorter-
dated options expiring in a month or longer-dated options expiring
in several years? Should they sell options that are close to or far away
from the current price of the commodity? Should they delta-hedge
their options or leave them unhedged? By delta hedging, investors
can limit their exposure to the direction of underlying price moves,
resulting in generally lower risk. However, the trade-off is that
delta hedging increases the transaction costs and reduces the return
potential. Unfortunately there is no right answer to these questions
that is guaranteed to produce the best returns, but there are some
guiding principles that can help in the pursuit of the best returns on
a risk-adjusted basis.

The simplest means of exploiting the richness in implied volatility is to use the options market to implement a particular price
view. For example, an investor might have reasonably strong conviction that the long-term price floor of oil will be $70 due to continued
emerging market demand growth and an increased need for less traditional, more costly production from sources such as tar sands and
deepwater wells. However, oil producers might need to limit their oil
price exposure should prices fluctuate below $70, their cost of new
production. Investors could sell $70 puts, since they should trade
"rich" to their fair value because of the demand from oil companies
seeking lower downside volatility on future profits. In this case, the
index investor is being paid to assume the risk that the oil company
is unwilling to take. Using an option selling strategy to take the
other side of producer hedging and earn income or gain additional
long exposure at a lower price is often a natural fit for index investors, who tend to be well-capitalized, long-term holders.

Exhibit 9-2 shows the average returns and information ratios
of several different option selling strategies on WTI crude oil
for multiple periods from 2000 to 2010. The top portion shows
the returns of selling one-month and three-month straddles

	Crude							
	1 Month				**3 Month**			
	Straddles		Strangles		Straddles		Strangles	
Period	Delta-Hedged	No Hedge	Delta-Hedged	No Hedge	Delta-Hedged	No Hedge	Delta-Hedged	No Hedge
1 mo. 0.25 yr	1.87%	2.99%	0.82%	3.51%	3.09%	−0.05%	3.16%	3.58%
	1.77%	4.78%	1.42%	3.96%	3.71%	8.78%	2.74%	5.73%
0.5 yr	1.90%	0.94%	1.97%	1.85%	3.73%	2.44%	3.00%	2.04%
1 yr	0.99%	0.53%	1.14%	1.86%	0.33%	−7.16%	−0.95%	−8.00%
2 yr	0.34%	0.10%	0.65%	1.04%	0.01%	−8.11%	−0.72%	−7.44%
3 yr	0.40%	0.14%	0.66%	0.80%	0.34%	−5.71%	−0.26%	−4.83%
5 yr	0.57%	0.30%	0.62%	0.74%	0.95%	−1.32%	0.34%	−1.68%
7 yr	0.59%	0.13%	0.64%	0.49%	0.86%	−1.11%	0.45%	−1.23%
10 yr	0.67%	0.44%	0.69%	0.72%	1.05%	−0.57%	0.60%	−0.62%
Period								
1 mo. 0.25 yr	4.75	10.50	8.10	35.32	3.67	2.01	7.70	6.13
0.5 yr	5.62	0.63	4.65	1.76	2.42	0.43	3.50	0.66
1 yr	1.00	0.25	1.80	1.46	0.08	−0.46	−0.30	−0.68
2 yr	0.40	0.05	1.04	0.75	0.00	−0.71	−0.32	−0.84
3 yr	0.55	0.08	1.23	0.62	0.14	−0.59	−0.14	−0.64
5 yr	0.88	0.18	1.39	0.65	0.49	−0.16	0.22	−0.27
7 yr	0.95	0.08	1.52	0.40	0.50	−0.15	0.33	−0.22
10 yr	1.05	0.26	1.65	0.60	0.64	−0.08	0.47	−0.12

Exhibit 9-2 **Average Profit (Premium Less Delta Hedging and Expiry Costs) per Trade in WTI Crude Oil as a Percentage of Notional**

Note: Periods shown relate to a given amount of time prior to March 31, 2010.

Source: Bloomberg, PIMCO, as of March 31, 2010

(at-the-money calls and puts), both with delta hedging and without delta hedging, and the same for one-month and three-month strangles (out-of-the-money puts and calls, with an initial delta of 0.25 in this example); the bottom portion shows the information ratios for each of these strategies.

The first main takeaway is that the information ratio, or return per unit of risk, is generally better when options are delta-hedged. Intuitively this makes sense because delta hedging helps reduce exposure to the movement in the underlying commodity price, which, in turn, provides a purer exposure to the difference between implied and realized volatility. Delta hedging is particularly important in commodity markets because supply and demand for most commodities is quite price inelastic in the short run, resulting in strongly trending price moves over short to intermediate time horizons. For example, while oil prices doubled from $70/barrel in July 2007 to $140/barrel in July 2008, demand for gasoline in the United States only declined by 2.5%. A very large price move, such as the doubling in oil prices from July 2007 to July 2008, would result in incredibly large losses from selling options without delta hedging. Contrast the results for delta hedging in commodities with those for delta hedging in equities, shown in Exhibit 9-3. In equities, delta hedging actually lowers the information ratio because equities typically lack the large trending moves seen in commodities, and they also appear to exhibit some tendency toward mean reversion over short time windows.

	S&P							
	1 Month				3 Month			
	Straddles		Strangles		Straddles		Strangles	
Period	Delta-Hedged	No Hedge	Delta-Hedged	No Hedge	Delta-Hedged	No Hedge	Delta-Hedged	No Hedge
1 mo.	1.11%	1.74%	1.57%	2.03%				
0.25 yr	1.19%	1.69%	0.89%	0.89%	2.01%	−6.12%	1.84%	−5.02%
0.5 yr	0.69%	1.25%	0.66%	1.45%	2.44%	−5.18%	2.28%	−3.10%
1 yr	−0.21%	0.69%	−0.34%	1.09%	−0.04%	−6.31%	−0.06%	−3.86%
2 yr	0.11%	1.20%	−0.04%	1.11%	0.30%	−1.39%	−0.19%	−0.87%
3 yr	0.03%	1.05%	0.02%	0.96%	0.27%	−0.98%	−0.07%	−0.61%
5 yr	0.15%	1.00%	0.13%	0.87%	0.68%	0.19%	0.25%	0.24%
7 yr	0.34%	1.06%	0.25%	0.91%	1.17%	1.34%	0.60%	0.93%
10 yr	0.34%	0.99%	0.23%	0.83%	1.04%	0.85%	0.50%	0.50%
Period								
1 mo.								
0.25 yr	3.53	1.46	4.71	1.42				
0.5 yr	1.79	1.61	2.30	3.06	8.10	−7.80	7.21	−2.28
1 yr	−0.26	0.48	−0.50	1.30	−0.02	−1.36	−0.03	−0.88
2 yr	0.19	1.04	−0.08	1.68	0.16	−0.32	−0.11	−0.26
3 yr	0.05	1.08	0.06	1.75	0.18	−0.27	−0.05	−0.22
5 yr	0.35	1.28	0.40	2.00	0.58	0.07	0.23	0.11
7 yr	0.89	1.44	0.87	2.27	1.08	0.49	0.61	0.48
10 yr	0.91	1.27	0.84	1.93	0.97	0.29	0.57	0.25

Exhibit 9-3 **Average Profit (Premium Less Delta Hedging and Expiry Costs) per Trade in S&P 500 as a Percentage of Notional**

Source: Bloomberg, PIMCO, as of March 31, 2010

The final point to note from the table of returns and information ratios (Exhibits 9-2 and 9-3) is that while there is no clear better choice between the returns of selling one-month and three-month options in crude oil, the information ratio of selling one-month options is generally higher. The reason for this has less to do with option theory and more to do with the law of large numbers.

Consider a variance swap, which is discussed in more detail below, and assume that an investor believes for certain that implied volatility is going to be 2 percentage points above realized volatility on average over the next year. The investor wants to make a profit of $2 million over the next year, or $1 million for every percentage point that realized volatility is below implied volatility. In option parlance, the investor will need $1 million of vega exposure (the dollar exposure for every percentage point change in volatility).

The investor considers two strategies: selling a one-year variance swap on $1 million of vega or selling one variance swap each month on one-twelfth of $1 million of vega. In both cases, the investor should make $2 million by the end of the year; however, the second case involves substantially lower volatility. For example, if implied volatility jumps from 30 to 40% the day after the investor strikes his one-year variance swap, he immediately incurs a mark-to-market loss of $10 million (10% on $1 million of vega). In the second case, the investor is exposed to only one-twelfth the vega, and thus his mark-to-market loss is only one-twelfth as large. While both strategies have the same expected absolute return, $2 million for the year, the risk-adjusted return of selling monthly or shorter-maturity variance swaps is far more attractive.

VARIANCE SWAPS

Delta-hedging many different option positions generally improves the information ratio of a short option position in commodities, but it involves considerable work and transaction costs. Fortunately, there is an alternative in the form of variance swaps. A variance swap gives direct exposure to the difference between the implied and realized

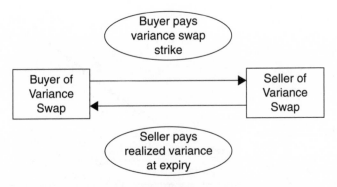

Exhibit 9-4 **Variance Swap Cash Flow Example**

Source: J.P. Morgan

volatility. Essentially, as Exhibit 9-4 shows, a variance swap involves one party (the buyer) paying implied volatility, referred to as the *strike*, and the other party (the seller) paying realized volatility.

The net payout from a variance swap is a function of the strike, denoted by K; the realized volatility, denoted by σ; and the notional, denoted by N. The payoff function for a variance swap is

$$\text{Payout} = N \times (\sigma^2 - K^2)$$

Variance swaps are typically traded in terms of vega, e.g., $100,000 of vega. For instance, a variance swap on $100,000 of vega will have a profit or loss of approximately $100,000 for each percentage point difference between the strike and the level of realized volatility. Expressing the payout in terms of vega, denoted by V, gives

$$\text{Payout} = \frac{V}{2K} \times (\sigma^2 - K^2)$$

While a thorough discussion of variance swaps is beyond the scope of this book, the main point to highlight regarding the variance swap payout is that it is nonlinear. When the level of realized volatility is close to the strike, the payout of a variance swap will be nearly linear, but as the level of realized volatility diverges from

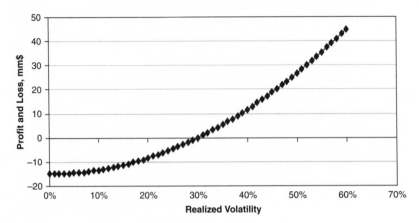

Exhibit 9-5 **Variance Swap Payoff**

Source: Illustration

the strike, the payout function becomes increasingly nonlinear. To illustrate this, Exhibit 9-5 shows the payout of a variance swap for a notional of $1 million vega and a strike of 30%. For levels of realized volatility near the strike, 30%, the payout function is nearly linear, and each percentage point change in realized volatility is equal to nearly a $1 million change in the payout; but as realized volatility starts to move significantly higher, each percentage point rise in realized volatility generates far more than an incremental $1 million profit.

Theoretically a variance swap can be decomposed into a basket of options that is delta-hedged each day. The weight for each option in the basket is determined so that the payout of the variance swap is only a function of the difference between the implied and realized volatility. The direction of price movements, either up or down, is irrelevant for the payout. This makes variance swaps an excellent tool for an index investor seeking to earn a return by selling "insurance" and capturing the spread between implied and realized volatility, because a variance swap avoids the uncertainty of taking exposure to outright directional price movements.

Since the complete replication of a variance swap requires a broad basket of options, variance swaps tend to trade primarily on commodities that have very liquid options markets—namely, gold, crude oil, natural gas, and to a lesser extent corn. Outside these markets, reduced liquidity and larger bid-ask spreads can make trading variance swaps less attractive. Variance swaps also frequently trade on indexes such as the DJUBSCI and S&P GSCI; however, these variance swap markets are generally more liquid for longer-maturity structures of several months to a few years, which corresponds to the terms of principal-protected notes.

The advantage of selling variance swaps on an index is that the index volatility includes some correlation assumption between the assets in the index; and just like volatility, correlation tends to trade rich. That is, the price of an option usually assumes a greater correlation between the commodities in the index than is actually realized. However, the disadvantage of selling index variance is that liquidity can be limited for shorter tenors. While longer-dated variance swaps should allow an investor to achieve similar returns and capture the same risk premium as shorter-dated variance swaps, as discussed earlier the information ratio of such a strategy tends to be lower due to less frequent resetting of the strike of the variance swap.

VARIANCE ON CRUDE OIL, GOLD, AND NATURAL GAS

Exhibit 9-6 shows the historical monthly payout of selling one-month variance swaps on a basket of gold, crude oil, and natural gas. For every $100 of vega, the basket is distributed 50% to gold, 30% to crude oil, and 20% to natural gas. The basket weights were constructed so that each commodity contributed a similar amount of risk to the basket; since gold volatility is less volatile than natural gas volatility, the basket has a larger vega exposure to gold than natural gas.

Exhibit 9-7 shows the cumulative payout for selling one-month variance swaps in gold, crude oil, natural gas, and the basket discussed above. Over the past 15 years there has been a meaningful positive return in all of these markets from structurally selling volatility, however there have been occasional large drawdowns. The annualized return of the variance swap basket has been $22.5 million per year for every $1 million of vega sold via variance swaps of

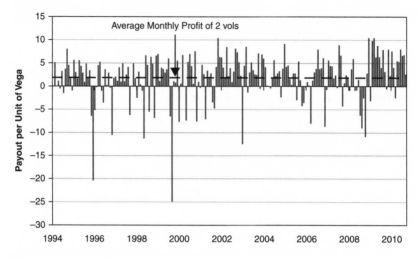

Exhibit 9-6 **Monthly Profit and Loss of Selling Variance on a Basket of Crude Oil, Gold, and Natural Gas**

Source: Bloomberg, PIMCO, as of October 31, 2010

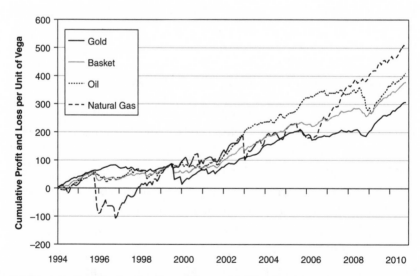

Exhibit 9-7 **Cumulative Profit and Loss of Selling Variance Swaps on Select Commodities**

Source: Bloomberg, PIMCO, as of July 31, 2010

one-month maturity. This strategy has historically realized a very strong information ratio of 1.28. However, like most insurance businesses, the key is both pricing your risk appropriately and, equally important, sizing your risk appropriately to be able to withstand the occasional very large losses.

As an aside, the annualized return from selling the variance swap basket discussed above implies the spread between the variance swap strike and realized volatility has averaged 1.88% ($22.5 million divided by $12 million of vega; $1 million vega was sold each month). The spread of 1.88% is less than the actual average difference between implied and realized volatility. Using the same data, the actual spread between implied and realized volatility was 2.66%. This difference between the actual spread of implied and realized volatility and the spread implied by the variance swap is a result of the nonlinear payout of a variance swap discussed previously. Since the payout of a short position in a variance swap is negatively convex, the seller of a variance swap experiences very large losses when volatility spikes and the level of realized volatility is far from the strike. These infrequent but large losses skew the average payout of a variance swap to be lower than the average spread between implied volatility and realized volatility. It is important to consider this nonlinear relationship when sizing the risk in selling variance swaps because most large losses occur when the variance swap strike is set quite low.

Even though historically it has been attractive to be a provider of insurance by selling variance swaps on a basket of commodities, the margin for error from inaccurate pricing or poor execution is typically small. Start with the average annual payout from selling $1 million of vega, $22.5 million per year. Assuming you sell variance swaps on the front contract in each of the commodities each month, that is an average monthly profit of $1.88 million, or a 1.88% difference between the strike and the realized volatility that is to be captured in each trade. Consider that the average bid-ask spread for a variance swap is between 1 and 3 percent. Demanding liquidity from the market and always executing on the bid side of the market could erode more than half the expected profits of a short variance strategy.

In addition to the bid-ask spread, the other risk in doing such a variance selling strategy is that counterparties may be less willing to show a fair bid if they believe that the person they are trading with is always going to be a seller. They may shade their market to try and extract as much profit as possible. This is why it is important to have an accurate ability to price such transactions. Just as auto insurance companies must have accurate risk models to calculate the appropriate rate for each driver, selling commodity variance swaps requires the ability to determine an appropriate price for a variance swap based upon the entire underlying strip of option prices. This helps an investor to determine when variance swaps are trading fair or rich to the underlying strip of options, or put another way, when an investor is providing or demanding liquidity from the market.

Proper sizing of risk is equally as important as correct pricing of risk. Selling volatility involves underwriting substantial risk. This is evidenced by Exhibits 9-6 and 9-8, which both show the

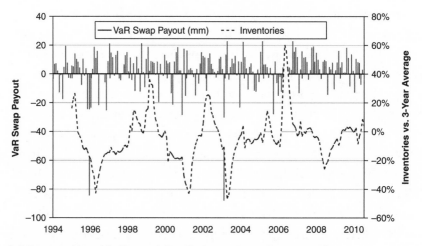

Exhibit 9-8 **Monthly Natural Gas Variance Swap Payout and Inventory Levels**

Source: Bloomberg, PIMCO, as of May 31, 2010

fat negative tail of the payout profile of a short variance strategy. There are many ways to try and quantify the risk in a short volatility strategy, and we will suggest two.

One method is to analyze the historic realized volatility of the payout for systematically selling variance swaps, which should be similar to the realized volatility of the implied-realized volatility spread, but with fatter tails given the convexity in variance swaps. In the case of our basket above, the annualized standard deviation of the monthly variance swap payout is $5.1 million per $1 million of vega. Given the fatter tails associated with selling volatility, sizing risk to be able to withstand a move of 4 to 5 standard deviations would be prudent. In this case, we should be prepared for a loss of $20–25 million per $1 million of vega.

The other way to size total risk would be to look at the maximum drawdown from historic moves in realized volatility. In the basket above, the maximum drawdown was $25 million, toward the higher end of our previous risk estimate. Suppose an investor were willing to lose a maximum of $2.5 million in selling variance; this would suggest that a maximum sizing of $0.1 million vega would be appropriate.

Throughout this discussion, we have used the example of selling variance on a basket of commodities because it is an excellent way to lower risk through diversification. The diversification benefit of the basket approach is apparent from looking at Exhibit 9-7, which shows the cumulative returns for the commodities individually as well as the total basket. Notice that the major drawdowns for the individual commodities do not occur at the same time; i.e., there is limited correlation between the implied-realized spread among these three commodities. In fact, the correlation for the monthly payout from selling variance swaps in each of these markets (gold, oil, and natural gas) is between 0 and 0.1. The basket's diversification benefit was particularly evident during the credit crisis in 2008. During 2008, realized volatility in oil went to above 100% as oil prices plunged more than $100 in five months as global growth slowed. However, during this time realized volatility in natural gas remained subdued, which helped to offset the losses experienced in crude oil.

There are also fundamental factors that are worthwhile to consider when assessing risk from selling volatility in commodity markets. For example, since inventories serve as a shock absorber for near-term supply-demand imbalances, periods of low inventories should be associated with increased price volatility as price is forced to bring supply and demand into balance. This exact phenomenon can be seen very clearly in natural gas. Exhibit 9-8 shows the payout from selling a one-month variance swap in natural gas each month along with inventories (measured as a percentage above or below the prior three-year average to remove seasonality). Notice that all of the top 5, and 8 of the top 10, monthly losses occurred when current-year inventories were below the average of the previous three years. In addition, the added tail risk from low inventories isn't compensated by above-average returns during these times. The average monthly gain when inventories are above their three-year average is $4.3 million, compared with an average loss of $0.2 million when inventories are below their three-year average. Tactically it makes sense to consider scaling risk back when selling natural gas volatility during periods of low inventory and to scale risk up when inventories are plentiful.

Hurricanes represent another major risk factor in selling natural gas variance. While this is definitely a large risk and should be considered in the scaling of positions, it has historically been less significant than the existence of low inventory levels. Hurricane Katrina, which severely impacted natural gas production in the Gulf of Mexico in August 2005, resulted in only the sixth largest loss from the variance selling strategy. Other major hurricanes to hit the gulf, such as Ivan in 2004 and Rita in 2005, produced only very small losses in the variance selling strategy. In all these cases, it appears that inventories fulfilled their objective, to serve as a shock absorber against extreme price moves.

Similar to natural gas, crude oil also shows a pattern of higher differences between implied and realized volatility at extreme levels of inventories. However, in crude oil, high levels of unanticipated volatility are noted when inventories are either very high or very low. In natural gas, the effect of high inventories is likely less pronounced because storage is filled throughout the year from April through October, and then storage is drawn down from November through March. Because of this cycling of storage, the only period where there is a real risk of maxing out natural gas storage occurs during a small window in October and November. For example, if storage is above average levels in June, the price can adjust gradually over a few months to adjust supply and demand before the storage overhang becomes a critical issue. However, in crude oil, if storage is near capacity and supply is above demand, then the market price of oil must fall in order to encourage incremental demand. Given the inelasticity of demand, the price may have to fall substantially. Because of this dynamic, the spread between implied and realized volatility is often more volatile and has fatter tails during periods with high levels of inventory than periods of low inventory.

Exhibit 9-9 shows the monthly payout from selling crude variance swaps along with the roll yield between the first and third crude oil contract. In crude oil, roll yield is used because it serves as a forward-looking measure for the level of inventories. When inventories are very high, the roll yield will be very negative, and when inventories are scarce, the roll yield will be positive. The exhibit shows that the majority of significant losses from selling volatility occurred during periods of either extreme contango or extreme backwardation. Just as in the case of natural gas, historically sellers of variance swaps in crude oil have not been not appropriately compensated during these periods of potentially elevated risk. The average return from selling $1 million of vega of crude oil variance over the 10% of months with the most backwardated roll yield was a loss of $1.1 million, and the average return over the

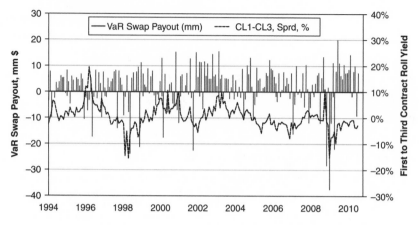

Exhibit 9-9 Monthly Variance Swap Payout and Crude Oil Roll Yield

Source: Bloomberg, PIMCO, as of March 31, 2010

10% of months that experienced the greatest contango was a profit of $0.8 million. These returns are substantially lower than the average profit of $2.6 million that was realized when the roll yield was not in either of these extreme ranges. In addition to lower average profitability when selling volatility at the extremes in inventory levels, the standard deviation is also larger. This increased tail risk should also be factored in during scaling of volatility sales, because being able to ride out inevitable storms is essential to any insurance or option selling strategy.

On average, while it is often profitable to sell options, the previous examples show that an understanding of current market fundamentals and basic market dynamics can meaningfully enhance return potential and both reduce and better quantify risk. In addition, given the size of the bid-ask spread and the exotic nature of variance swaps, having a robust pricing model is imperative for assessing value. When combined, these elements result in a successful framework to help enhance commodity index returns by focusing on extracting risk premium from the commodities options market.

Having discussed various structural sources of potential out-performance in commodity markets that an intelligent indexer can exploit, we turn in the next few chapters to the actual implementation of these strategies. In particular, we discuss briefly another rich source of structural outperformance—the intelligent investment of the collateral pool of fixed-income securities that underlies the commodity futures exposure. We also discuss risk management both in terms of philosophy and in terms of technology.

CHAPTER 10

Implementation

We have spent several chapters discussing the dynamics of various commodity markets and indexes and offered suggestions on ways to systematically take advantage of inefficiencies or mispricing in these markets. In this chapter and the next, we outline the actual implementation and subsequent monitoring and management of these positions. We spend the bulk of this chapter discussing, with the help of real-world examples, implementation for practitioners. We first focus on implementation of the commodity exposure, where liquidity, confidentiality, and best available market pricing—as well as the desire for customized payoff profiles—may lead to implementation via swaps, futures, or options. We then switch our focus to the other half of commodity index investing, namely, the management of the collateral underlying the commodity exposure. We discuss several "structural" sources of outperformance over the simple T-bill collateral used by most published commodity indexes. Accurate and prudent risk management of both active commodity and collateral positions is an integral part of intelligent commodity indexing. We discuss this in the next chapter.

COMMODITY ALPHA TRADE IMPLEMENTATION

There are two complementary frameworks or philosophies for intelligent commodity index replication. The first one is to build up positions that make up an "intelligent" index in an effort to track and outperform a published index. This involves first using some of the strategies discussed in the previous chapters to identify the particular commodities and contracts on each curve that give the most efficient exposure to a given index and then managing and rolling these positions as needed. Alternatively, one could "outsource" the beta exposure or the naive index replication to a specialist commodity index replication operation that has the economies of scale and resources to offer cheap passive index replication. This second approach can allow an investor to focus solely on alpha trades that are designed to neutralize the suboptimal portions of the index, replacing these with more attractive alternatives. A simple example would serve to illustrate these two economically equivalent approaches to intelligent commodity index investing.

Assume that the S&P GSCI holds its WTI crude oil exposure in the June 2011 contract (CLM1), and the WTI crude oil curve is in contango in the front months due to an excess of inventory at the delivery point in Cushing, Oklahoma. This means that in May 2011, a passive index investor would need to roll this exposure into the July 2011 contract (CLN1), buying CLN1 at a higher-dollar price than the price at which the CLM1 was sold. An intelligent indexer may prefer to hold the exposure in the June 2012 futures contract (CLM2), a year further out, where the WTI crude oil curve is in backwardation. As discussed in Chapter 6, "Maximizing Roll Yield," in a situation where nothing changes, it is economically more advantageous to hold a futures position when the curve is backwardated (positive roll yield) than when it is in contango (negative roll yield). Moreover, the investor may expect a recovering economy along with the construction of new pipelines to carry oil out of Cushing to resolve the oversupply, but these may be at least a year away, and so the contango could persist. The two complementary (and economically equivalent) ways of implementing this view are to either (1)

purchase CLM2 rather than CLM1 for the WTI crude oil portion
of the S&P GSCI or (2) obtain passive exposure to the entire S&P
GSCI and then overlay this exposure with a curve trade that is long
CLM2 versus short CLM1. The first approach has the advantage
of being less balance-sheet intensive and more intuitive, while the
second allows the separation of the low value-added beta component
from the higher value-added alpha component. As we further discuss below, both these approaches could be implemented either in
the listed futures market or in the OTC swap market.

Two broad classes of instruments are available to investors
looking to get the kind of derivative-based exposure to commodity
markets discussed in this book. The first is via "listed," or exchange-
traded, instruments such as futures; and the second is via "nonlisted,"
or OTC, products, namely swaps. Finally, sometimes cheaper exposure and more optimal payoff profiles are obtained via options on
commodities. Option-based strategies can also be executed in either
listed or OTC format.

IMPLEMENTING WITH FUTURES

Futures are the most liquid and transparent way to get exposure to
the front-end contracts of the various commodity curves. Moreover,
since futures are exchange-traded, they have substantially reduced
counterparty risk, given the efficient margining requirements along
with the capital and insurance policies of the futures clearing mer-
chant (FCM). In addition, the exchange itself stands between the
investor and his or her counterpart on the trade. A schematic showing the different participants and cash flows involved in a futures
trade is shown in Exhibit 10-1.

Although the level of guarantee and safeguard varies from
exchange to exchange, the guarantees and safeguards are sufficiently
rigorous at the major commodity exchanges to protect most investors from loss due to counterparty default. For example, the Chicago
Mercantile Exchange (CME) implements several layers of protection
against counterparty default. These protections include an audit of
the financials and risk management practice of each FCM. Moreover,

Exhibit 10-1 Schematic of Counterparty Exposure for a Futures Trade

the CME itself is the counterparty to the FCM for every position held. The CME implements twice-a-day mark-to-market and variation margin settlement during normal times, and it has the right to do so more often during volatile periods. Segregation of FCM and client accounts is designed to protect against default by the FCM. In addition, there is recourse to a $100 million surplus fund when normal clearing activity does not resolve obligations in the case of an FCM default, and there is also recourse to at least another $2.3 billion (as of June 2010) aggregate guarantee fund posted from non-defaulting FCMs. Thus, the possibility of loss due to counterparty default in an exchange-traded transaction is reduced. However, as the recent bankruptcy of MF Global illustrates (see Exhibit 10-1), exchange cleared transactions are not completely risk free, and counterparty due diligence remains vital in spite of the safeguards discussed above.

The other advantage of implementation in the futures markets is that most commodity futures trading is now electronic, and hence confidentiality is assured. Perhaps the only major drawback of implementing commodity exposure via futures contracts is the lack of liquidity further out the curve. As Exhibits 10-2 and 10-3 show, open interest for WTI crude oil and Henry Hub natural gas futures drops dramatically as one goes out more than two years. Other markets like corn and wheat see even larger liquidity declines out the curve. Liquidity in the listed contracts for most commodities is generally adequate out to one year but can be limited further out the curve. Views on shapes or levels of commodity curves in the distant future can be difficult to implement using listed futures. This is because most of the large long-term hedging transactions by physical commodity producers and consumers are implemented in the OTC markets; thus investors who wish to avail themselves of this liquidity to express their views must be willing to move away from listed futures in order to do so.

Finally, we should point out that there exist listed futures contracts not just on individual commodities, but also on certain commodity indexes like the S&P GSCI and the DJUBSCI. However,

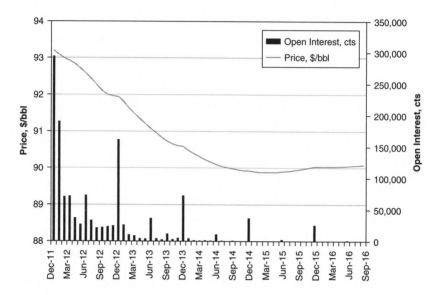

Exhibit 10-2 NYMEX WTI Crude Oil Price Curve and Open Interest

Source: Bloomberg, as of October 31, 2011

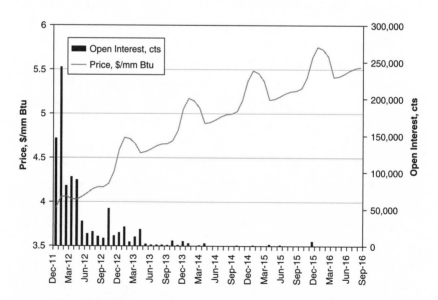

Exhibit 10-3 NYMEX Natural Gas Price Curve and Open Interest

Source: Bloomberg, as of October 31, 2011

	Open Interest, mm $	Daily Volume, mm $	Annual Roll Cost,* bps
S&P GSCI Futures	2,257	94	30–45
DJUBSCI Futures	151	3	30–45
S&P GSCI Underlying Futures	102,526	36,252	10–15
DJUBSCI Underlying Futures	51,879	17,801	10–15

Exhibit 10-4   **A Comparison of the Relative Liquidity and Cost of Index Futures Versus Underlying Index Constituents**

*The annual roll cost is based upon a typical bid-ask spread for each futures roll.

Note: The index length in underlying futures is calculated by taking the open interest of each market divided by the index weight. The smallest value across all commodities is taken as the size available.

Source: PIMCO, Bloomberg, as of June 30, 2011

at the time of this writing, these futures are both fairly illiquid and expensive to buy and roll relative to the underlying indexes, as Exhibit 10-4 illustrates. Hence they are not currently an efficient means of getting long beta-type exposure to commodities. Exhibit 10-4 compares the relative liquidity and cost of the underlying constituents of the DJUBSCI and S&P GSCI futures as well as the futures contracts that trade on the DJUBSCI and the S&P GSCI. The first two rows shown are for the DJUBSCI and S&P GSCI futures, while the next two cover the index constituents. The open interest for the futures that make up the index is orders of magnitude more liquid than the index contract. In addition to better liquidity, there is also lower cost in the underlying futures. The upside of using futures based upon the indexes is their simplicity. An investor can replicate an index with just one index futures contract, compared with roughly 20 or more contracts if using the underlying futures that make up the index.

IMPLEMENTING WITH SWAPS

An investor can use the OTC swap market to implement positions in individual commodities as well as on indexes. In the case of single commodities, the most commonly used type of swap references the

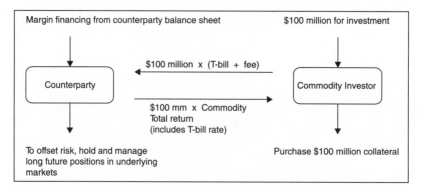

Exhibit 10-5 **Schematic of Cash Flows and Exposures Involved in an OTC Commodity Total Return Swap**

underlying futures contract and is financially settled based on the closing price of the referenced contract a few days before the last trading date of the contract. A swap contract is functionally similar to a futures contract in that one of the counterparties has "long" exposure to the underlying commodity or index and the other side has "short" exposure, as illustrated in Exhibit 10-5. One big difference is that both counterparties are exposed to a default by the other, and another big difference is that there is not an exchange or FCM standing as a guarantor between them (similar to futures contracts; however, swaps typically start with zero economic exposure between counterparties and entail regular exchange of margin to account for mark-to-market gains or losses).

An advantage of swaps is that they can be customized as needed with terms including threshold, frequency, and type of collateral that can be posted for margin. For example, a tax-sensitive investor may choose to post high-rated municipal bonds as margin against a commodity position. Swaps may or may not require the posting of initial margin; the terms of this are negotiated between the two counterparties. On the other hand, futures, which are traded on an exchange, have a standardized initial margin requirement.

Since swaps are individually negotiated, they can be almost infinitely customized to reference, for example, specific baskets of commodities with client-specified rules for maturities, roll periods, weights, etc. The customization can include detailed specifications of obligations in the event of a default or ratings downgrade of the broker-dealer and conversely the maximum amount of leverage or the maximum notional of exposure allowed in the investor's account. Starting in 2012, as the requirements of the Dodd-Frank legislation start to be implemented, it is likely that many swaps will be exchange-cleared and hence, at least in their simplest form, will start to resemble futures even more strongly.

IMPLEMENTING WITH OPTIONS

Finally, there are situations where implementing a position via options (either listed or OTC) may be the most efficient means of expressing a view. This is typically the case when consumers, producers, or even investors are looking for leverage or off-balance-sheet exposure to commodities.

In general, liquidity for options is usually better in the OTC markets than in the listed markets. This is simply a function of where most of the large flows take place. Consumers and producers hedging in the options markets are often in long-dated maturities or have complicated payout structures that are just not available in the listed options contracts. Investment banks on the other side of these flows will typically look to hedge themselves in the underlying markets or lay off the risk to other investors. This is often where intelligent index investors can find attractive opportunities to express views or enhancements to their index positions.

We use a couple of examples to illustrate the use of options to get outright exposure to commodity markets or to express more nuanced views on the relative prices of two or more commodities. Here we restrict the discussion to vanilla options. There is an almost infinitely customizable set of payoff profiles that one can devise for options—more often than not, these are better suited for higher-frequency traders who can actively manage the risk of these positions.

Consider the recent situation where high-net-worth individuals are obtaining exposure to the commodity markets via structured notes sold by various banks. These notes are typically sold with an embedded put that helps protect the investor from the downside in the commodity markets (principal-protected notes). A result of the large number of such notes sold is that the banking community is short puts on commodity indexes, and they are often willing to pay a premium to buy them back. This is why the implied volatility in the commodity index option market tends to trade above realized volatility on average (see Exhibit 10-6). The higher level of implied volatility relative to realized volatility means the options on average trade above fair value. In this case, one says the puts on the commodity index are trading rich. In such a situation, an investor could get exposure to the commodity index by selling these rich puts to the banking community. This approach is particularly applicable if commodity indexes have been rallying and an investor would like to get exposure in the case of

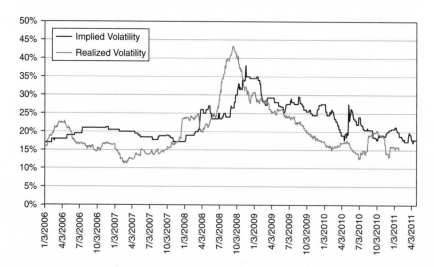

Exhibit 10-6 Implied and Realized Volatility on the DJUBSCI, Three-Month Tenor

Source: PIMCO, Bloomberg, Goldman Sachs, as of April 30, 2011

a pull-back but does not want to chase the market in the case of a rally. By selling, say, 10% out-of-the money puts, the investor will get long the index in the case of a 10% sell-off, but he or she will have no exposure and keep the option premium if the index sells off less than 10% (or rallies).

Another example of gaining exposure via options is in the oil market. The price of WTI crude oil severely underperformed the rally in Brent crude oil during the first part of 2011 due to a glut of oil in the U.S. midcontinent around Cushing, Oklahoma. This caused many investors to prefer gaining long exposure to Brent crude oil because they believed it better represented global supply and demand fundamentals. The market priced WTI at a sizable discount to Brent out many years.

Assuming investors wanted to express the view that this dislocation would prove temporary and resolve itself over the next couple of years, then they could simply buy deferred futures contracts in WTI and sell deferred futures contracts in Brent. However, the same view could also be implemented in the options market. To go long WTI and short Brent, investors would buy WTI calls and sell Brent calls. The options would only have value if the price of oil rose, and they would be worthless if the price of oil declined. Therefore, such a structure would be particularly attractive if an investor particularly wanted this exposure in a rising price environment. The primary motivation, in this instance, to put on the trade using options is because longer maturity Brent call options were trading rich to WTI call options; i.e., the implied volatility was higher in Brent than in WTI. Exhibit 10-7 shows the difference between Brent and WTI realized volatility, and historically WTI has averaged higher volatility than Brent due to the constraints of the Cushing delivery point for WTI. There is no fundamental reason the realized volatility of Brent prices should be higher than that of WTI prices, however the implied volatility of Brent options can be higher than WTI due to imbalances in the supply and demand in the options market.

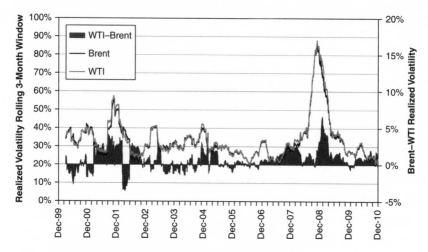

Exhibit 10-7 Brent and WTI Rolling Front-Month Contracts

Source: PIMCO, Bloomberg, as of December 31, 2010

The richness of the Brent options was a result of hedge funds and other investors buying call options on oil in order to gain exposure to a rise in crude prices. There were lots of buyers of Brent call options but few buyers of WTI call options. Specifically, in early 2011, the December 13 WTI contract was trading at $107 and the December 13 Brent contract was trading at $114, a spread of $7. In options, it was possible to buy a $120 call on WTI and sell a $131 call on Brent for no cost. This means that in the futures market the investor could go long the spread at $7, but in the options market the investor could go long the spread at $11. In the options market the investor could effectively get a $4 head start due to the richness of the Brent options.

IMPLEMENTING AND MANAGING THE COLLATERAL PORTFOLIO

Most index investors have a fully funded collateral portfolio—backing every dollar of commodity exposure with a dollar of high-quality collateral. As discussed earlier, this is because they view the investment, not as a speculative investment to be leveraged, but rather as a fundamental asset allocation decision in order to hedge against inflation and diversify their investments in traditional financial instruments.

Given this motivation, one of the key decisions that a commodity index investor has to make, and a potent source for enhancing return potential, is the choice and management of the collateral underlying the commodity exposure (whether implemented via futures, options, or swaps). Most commodity indexes invest all their cash collateral in three-month T-bills. In our opinion, there is nothing particularly intelligent in investing all the collateral in one of the safest, most liquid, and hence lowest-yielding securities in the world. Three-month T-bills in 2011 were yielding a paltry 0.05% per year. It may be reasonable to use this T-bill rate in publishing an index, since the index provider does not want to bring other risks, such as fixed-income risk, into the index performance. But in implementation, actually using T-bills is an inefficient use of capital. In our opinion, going forward, T-bills are unlikely to provide a positive real return because central banks will keep policy rates at low levels to stimulate consumption and investment as well as boost asset prices. Hence, going forward, T-bills are likely to detract from the inflation-hedging properties of a generic commodity index rather than enhance it. In this environment, we believe it is more important than ever to actively manage the collateral portion of a commodity index investment.

After setting aside a prudent amount of T-bills for liquidity and margin requirements, it is possible to add value and enhance the returns over that of a passive index by active management of the collateral pool (the appropriate amount of liquidity will be addressed in the next chapter on risk management). One way to do this is by exploiting certain recurrent risk premiums in fixed-income markets, similar to the structural trades we have discussed in the commodity markets. In addition to these structural sources of outperformance over T-bills, an experienced investor should be able to add additional value by having views on the direction of interest rates, careful security selection, etc. Exhibit 10-8 provides examples of some of these structural and tactical methods of enhancing collateral returns, and the following paragraphs provide several brief real-life examples.

Investors in fixed-income markets typically demand compensation for maturity, liquidity, credit, and volatility risks. Extending the maturity of the collateral pool from three months typically increases the yield, as does the purchase of securities that may be just slightly less liquid than T-bills. A recent example occurred after the crisis of 2008 with the introduction of the Temporary Liquidity Guarantee Program (TLGP). Under this program, certain financial entities were allowed to issue short-maturity bonds that were backed by the Federal Deposit Insurance Corporation. The bonds issued by banks under the TLGP are essentially corporate bonds backed by the full faith and credit of the U.S. government. At the initiation of this program, it was possible to buy bonds that were nearly identical in credit quality to T-bills but that offered yields up to 100 bps higher.

Another alternative is to invest in short-maturity government bonds of foreign issuers (which may have a stronger fiscal position than the United States) that yield more than T-bills, even after the currency is hedged. For example, Australian banks issued USD-denominated bonds backed by the full faith and credit of the Australian government under a program equivalent to the TLGP. Sometimes it is possible to take advantage of imbalances in the currency markets to purchase government bills that may look optically lower in yield than T-bills but yield more after the currency component is hedged out. (This involves giving up some liquidity, as they must be held to maturity to earn this additional "basis" premium). With the appropriate credit analysis, one can find securities that are not backed by the full faith and credit of the U.S. government but yet are highly unlikely to default (or better yet are backed by underlying assets that can be recovered in the case of a default). There are numerous possibilities to safely earn a yield greater than T-bills.

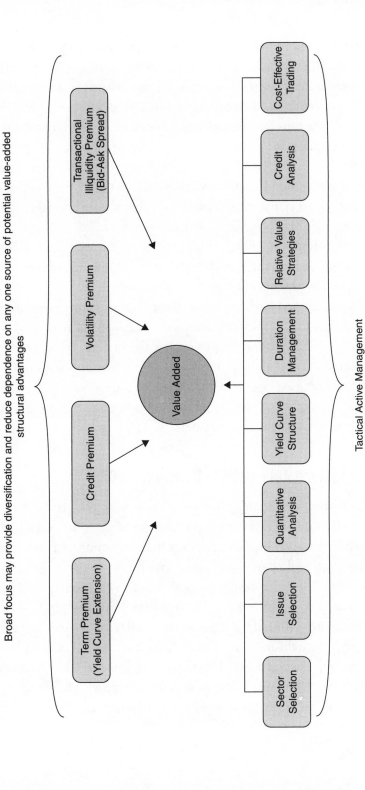

Broad focus may provide diversification and reduce dependence on any one source of potential value-added structural advantages

Term Premium (Yield Curve Extension)

Credit Premium

Volatility Premium

Transactional Illiquidity Premium (Bid-Ask Spread)

Value Added

Sector Selection

Issue Selection

Quantitative Analysis

Yield Curve Structure

Duration Management

Relative Value Strategies

Credit Analysis

Cost-Effective Trading

Tactical Active Management

Exhibit 10-8 **Adding Value and Enhancing Returns in the Collateral Portion of a Commodity Portfolio**

Finally, many fixed-income securities come with embedded options that are occasionally mispriced by the markets. An example of this type of bond is an agency callable bond issued by an agency of the U.S. government, such as Fannie Mae. A callable bond gives the issuer the option to buy a bond back if rates are lower in the future. If rates are lower, the price of the bond will rise, but the issuer has the right to buy the bond back at par. Essentially, this makes the holder of such a bond short a call option, and the investor receives a higher interest rate to compensate for being short this call option. To the extent this option is mispriced by the market, it is possible that these option-embedded bonds can add incremental return even after accounting for the possibility that the embedded option may be exercised by the borrower.

As mentioned earlier, if sufficient fixed-income expertise is available, one can tactically manage the collateral portfolio rather than just statically attempting to exploit the various sources of risk premium discussed above. One can actively express views on the direction of interest rates, credit spreads, volatility, and relative performance of different sectors of the bond market in an effort to boost returns via the collateral pools.

PRODUCTS AVAILABLE TO INDIVIDUAL INVESTORS

Before closing, we should talk about two investment products that allow individual investors to gain commodity index exposure: open-end mutual funds and ETFs. Open-end mutual funds that invest in commodity indexes come in many forms (intelligent and not so), and they also track many different commodity indexes. The advantage of these funds is that they have the potential to give the investor intelligent commodity indexing in one package. Open-end mutual funds are all run differently, and managers have different objectives and skill levels; but in general, the collateral can be managed in instruments beyond the basic T-bill holdings assumed by the index. In addition, the manager can deviate from the published commodity index in order to enhance returns. Such deviations will likely include many of the strategies discussed in this book, such as rolling on different days and holding different contracts than the index holds as well as looking at substitution and relative value across the commodities universe. The disadvantage is the standard structure of the open-end mutual fund, where redemptions and subscriptions are only accepted once a day at the closing price. However, such a restriction should not be a major impediment for long-term investors.

ETFs typically passively invest in either a commodity index or a single commodity. These trade on equity exchanges. They can be traded throughout the day like individual stocks, and they often trade at a discount or a premium to their underlying net asset value. Moreover, just like they can for single stocks, investors can buy and sell options on the prices of these commodity ETFs.

Note that many of the securities that look like ETFs on commodity indexes are actually exchange-traded notes, ETNs. One way that ETNs differ from ETFs is in their tax treatment. Also, unlike ETFs, ETNs do not have the typical tracking error to a published benchmark. Instead ETNs have credit risk to the issuer of the ETN. For example, the ETN issued on the S&P GSCI is a debt instrument issued by Barclays Bank. Barclays Bank guarantees that the instrument will have the same performance of the S&P GSCI. However, holders of ETNs do not own underlying futures contracts or other collateral; instead they own debt issued by Barclays Bank.

This chapter discussed the various means of implementing an intelligent commodity indexing strategy, focusing on the commodities as well as collateral that make up an index. We ended with a brief discussion of the products available to individual investors. Equally important in the implementation of intelligent commodity index strategies is the risk management that makes sure this is a viable long-term strategy. We discuss this in the next chapter.

CHAPTER 11

Risk Management

Managing the risk of commodity positions and commodity indexes is a multifaceted effort. Investors are faced with the fact that they are using derivatives to get exposure to the prices of volatile assets, whose underlying physical availability or supply and demand depends on weather and geopolitical considerations in addition to the standard economic factors. Moreover, we are dealing in derivatives with strictly regulated (and currently uncertain) reporting rules. Hence risk management involves both manager common sense and focus, supported by sophisticated technology and systems. The systems should, at a minimum, allow one to monitor:

- Delivery risk (the risk of being forced to either make delivery or accept delivery of physical commodities, as well as the risk of changing delivery requirements)
- Market risk (the risk of adverse price movements)
- Counterparty risk (the risk of insolvency for derivatives' counterparties and clearinghouses)
- Regulatory and reporting risk (risk that positions are not compliant with regulations and that reporting is tardy or inaccurate)

Most investors' risk systems are set up to deal only with market risk; and even here they may not have the granularity to deal with commodity markets, where contracts with maturities just a month apart can behave very differently depending on the proximity to delivery periods and planting or harvest seasons.

Commodity markets are given to sharp price spikes and declines that are more frequent than the normal distribution used in standard statistical analysis would indicate. As an illustration, Exhibit 11-1 shows the tails of a normal distribution versus the daily log returns of the front-month WTI oil futures contract for the past 10 years. In general, a 3-sigma move, equivalent to a daily price change of roughly 6%, is nearly three times as likely in the oil market as the normal distribution would suggest.

The fat tails of the distribution of commodity prices are largely a result of commodity demand being price inelastic in the short term combined with unexpected supply-side disruptions. Disruptions to commodity supply can be caused by numerous factors, including adverse weather, terrorism, civil strife, natural disasters, geopolitical

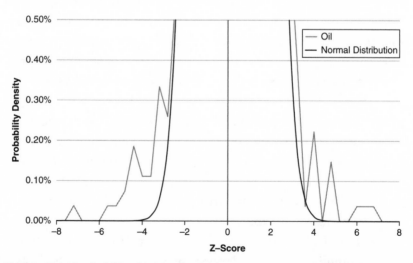

Exhibit 11-1   **Probability Density for Daily Log Returns in Oil Compared with Normal Distribution**

Source: Bloomberg, PIMCO, as of December 31, 2010

actions, human error, etc. In addition to supply and demand dynamics causing larger-than-expected price moves, waves of deleveraging where speculative positions are unwound simultaneously can also lead to sharp and disorderly declines in commodity prices. Even if only temporary, until fundamental economic factors can again take hold, this potential price volatility is a risk that must be managed ... or the investor might not survive to see the long-term return of stability. Such deleveraging episodes can be driven by macroeconomic data releases or by other factors such as an increase in margin levels caused by the exchange lowering the availability of credit. Positions should thus be sized relative to the ability of an investor to handle drawdowns that are often sharper and more frequent than predicted by standard statistical models. Scenario analysis allowing a stressing of prices and correlation is an integral part of risk management for commodity positions.

Moreover, to the extent that intelligent commodity indexing includes the active management of collateral backing commodity exposure (see Chapter 10, "Implementation"), the risk management framework and technology must also cover fixed-income risk. The risk of a failure to implement prudent collateral management practices cannot be overstated. The events of 2008 clearly demonstrated this when more than one commodity index fund was forced to close, not because there were sharp declines in the commodity markets, but rather because the liquidity and credit profiles of the underlying collateral portfolios were not well understood! Finally, counterparty risk management is extremely important because derivatives-based strategies invariably involve exposure to a counterparty who promises to pay off (settle) the economic value of a position at some future date.

DISAGGREGATING INDEXES

Given the above risks, what are some of the specifics that a robust commodity risk management paradigm must contain? The first, and most basic, requirement is to know exactly what your underlying exposure is; i.e., you need an accurate accounting of exposure by individual commodity and by maturity. For example, it is not enough to know just the total notional amount of crude oil owned. One must know exactly how many contracts, across which months or years, of what grade, and whether these are listed (and if so, on what exchange) or OTC. Getting to this level of detail with direct futures exposure or even single commodity swaps is straightforward. However, to the extent that positions include swaps that reference a basket of commodities or a commodity index, these positions need to be disaggregated into their individual underlying exposures. Hence, each commodity index swap entered into the position management system should have enough accompanying data fields (weights of different commodities, contract reference months, rules for rolling positions) to allow for a complete disaggregation into individual commodity futures contracts.

This is also true if the investor uses an aggregated commodity index futures contract. Full specification requires input from the trader up front for nonstandard commodity baskets or index swaps—this is essential for proper position and risk management. The risk management system should be set up so that specifying the reference commodities, their weights, their roll dates, and any dynamic rebalancing rules (based on curve shapes, relative prices, etc.) allows a complete disaggregation of a swap into its component commodities. The example in Exhibit 11-2 shows how $100 million invested on May 3, 2011, in a total return swap that references the DJ-UBS index can be decomposed into its underlying components. When a portfolio grows increasingly complex, with various different custom indexes consisting of several different contracts that all roll on different dates, the type of disaggregation shown in Exhibit 11-2 can be used to give a clear sense of the risk in the portfolio relative to the benchmark and how the risk evolves over time.

Commodity	Bloomberg Ticker	Contract	Contracts
Crude Oil	CL	CLN1	147
Heating Oil	HO	HON1	30
Gasoline	XB	XBN1	30
Natural Gas	NG	NGN1	228
Gold	GC	GCM1	68
Silver	SI	SIN1	20
Copper	HG	HGN1	62
Aluminum	LA	LAN1	74
Nickel	LN	LNN1	14
Zinc	LX	LXN1	42
Corn	C	C N1	208
Soybeans	S	S N1	102
Wheat	W	W N1	104
Live Cattle	LC	LCM1	70
Lean Hogs	LH	LHM1	56
Coffee	KC	KCN1	24
Sugar	SB	SBN1	88
Cocoa	CC	CCN1	0
Cotton	CT	CTN1	25
Soybean Oil	BO	BON1	76

Exhibit 11-2 **Disaggregation of an Index Total Return Swap**

Source: PIMCO. Sample for illustrative purposes only.

MANAGING DELIVERY RISK

Setting up systems to monitor the delivery window for various commodities as well as appropriate reporting to regulators is straightforward once all positions (swaps, futures, options) are known at the atomic level. As an example, at PIMCO the portfolio managers, risk managers, and operations personnel are alerted automatically when any commodity is within five days of its first notice date or last trade date (whichever comes first). These groups continue to be notified until the position is closed or rolled or

Monitor all outstanding futures positions relative to delivery dates			
Pimco Ticker	Long Qty.	Short Qty.	Days Until Delivery/Notified
CAK1	95	0	8
LAK1	62	0	14
LNK1	76	0	14
LLK1	0	−94	14
LPK1	0	−24	14
LXK1	0	−67	14
CLM1	801	0	18
GCM1	2	0	29
XBM1	2	0	29

Exhibit 11-3 **Futures Delivery Monitor**
Source: PIMCO, as of May 2, 2011

the portfolio managers decide to take delivery of the underlying commodity. Such a system requires that delivery and trading schedules for all positions that entail physical delivery are stored in the system. In addition, delivery and trading schedules for financially settled positions are also stored, but these have a different protocol than that for commodities that require physical settlement. A stylized example of such a delivery risk management report is shown in Exhibit 11-3.

Having the disaggregated or atomic-level commodity positions along with historical market prices and correlations allows one to build an intuitive and flexible risk system. The risk system can produce standard risk measures such as tracking error or value at risk (VaR), but it is also flexible enough to run scenario analysis based upon hypothetical or historic periods to estimate the impact on the portfolio for different changes in prices, curve shapes, volatilities, and correlations. However, prudent risk management and position sizing start well before a trade is executed, let alone before it is picked up by the risk management system. This should include not just the expected VaR of the trade in consideration, but also estimates of the maximum expected drawdown as well as correlation with other positions already in the portfolio.

SIZING OF TRADES

Every new trade is initiated with the expectation of making money. However, in sizing a trade, one should take into account the conviction level, statistical measures of the volatility or probability of loss (tracking error or VaR), and also correlation with existing positions in the portfolio (does it add to or reduce overall risk?). Finally, one should also include an estimate of the maximum drawdown of the trade, based partly on historic results but also with an eye for what could be different this time. For example, a 10% long WTI–short Brent position expecting mean reversion put on in 2010 would have estimated a less than 1% chance of the spread moving out beyond more than $5, or roughly 5% of the price of oil. Ex-ante with the spread at $3, the investor would estimate only a 1% chance of losing more than 20 bps (2% times a 10% position). A historical analysis on maximum drawdown would have shown that the widest the spread could trade was $10, or a loss of 70 bps. However, all these measures ultimately underestimated the risk, as the spread traded out past $20 in 2011. Widening from $3 to $20 would have resulted in a loss of 170 bps, nearly 8 times the ex-ante estimate using a 99% confidence interval.

Correlations Matter

Every portfolio manager has a maximum risk budget, whether self-imposed, client-imposed, or management-imposed. Care should be taken so that no single trade either expectedly or unexpectedly, as in the example above, dominates this risk budget. This risk budget should be distributed over a number of trades, allocating a larger portion to the high-conviction trades and a smaller portion to the low-conviction trades. In addition, trades that provide greater diversification benefits should also be given larger weightings because they will help to improve the overall risk-return profile of the portfolio. It is important when constructing a portfolio to consider correlations because seemingly distinct trades could be highly correlated and have significant exposure to a single risk factor, resulting in an imprudent allocation of risk. For example, consider the following four seemingly different trades (with hypothetically very different rationales):

1. Going short crude oil. Crude at the top of its recent trading range; expect mean reversion.
2. Going long deferred crude oil versus nearby crude oil. Optimize roll yield in a contango market.
3. Selling crude oil variance. Implied volatility trading rich to realized due to producer hedging programs.
4. Going long gasoline cracks. Refinery margins near lows; expect refiners to cut runs and support margins.

In the case of a supply disruption, either related to weather or caused by a geopolitical event, the price of oil would obviously rise. In addition, the curve would move to greater backwardation due to a shortage of inventories, and volatility would rise since uncertainty about the supply of oil has increased. Finally, refinery margins would be compressed because of the short-term lag in product prices as refiners attempt to pass on the higher input prices to end users. All these trades contained one common risk factor, a sharp move in the price of oil. What seemed to be four well-thought-out, separate trades was actually just one money losing trade!

In order to address this problem, an intelligent index investor, when sizing a trade, will look at correlations in four different ways:

1. Current realized correlations (with some standard time window for look-back and decay factors)
2. Realized correlations during time periods when markets were exceptionally stressed or volatile
3. Forward-looking correlations using an algorithm that produces a positive definite variance-covariance matrix using historical inputs as a guide and user-defined correlations for as many commodity pairs as desired
4. The extreme case where all correlations move to 1.0

POSITION MANAGEMENT

Once a trade is initiated, the focus shifts to ongoing risk management. The risk and position management system should be built to provide a mix of an intuitive high-level view and a more detailed and granular view. The top-level view should be intuitive enough so that a risk manager or an experienced investment professional can get a quick idea of where the main risks are and a numeric estimate of the scale of these risks. In addition, there need to be increasingly granular views for specialists that focus on the microstructure of the portfolio. These multiple views, ultimately getting down to the level of individual commodities and contracts, are an important tool for specialists looking to maximize the diversification across the portfolio. The example in Exhibit 11-4 gives a graphical representation of one realization of such a position and risk management system.

At the top level of Exhibit 11-4, the risk system shows deviations from the index in terms of the broad commodity sectors, broken into wide-maturity segments. This particular example chooses to show deviations versus the benchmark in terms of percentage of market value. Drop-down choices allow one to display the deviations in terms of notional amounts, number of contract equivalents, tracking error, VaR, or any of a number of other risk measures. In the exhibit, the investor is 5% overweight the Oil/Products sector, and exposure is concentrated in the three-month–six-month bucket.

From this top-level risk view, it is possible to drill down further to get a more micro view of the risk in the portfolio. For example, drilling down into the Oil/Products class shows a breakdown by commodity within that sector along with more granular maturity bucketing. While there is an overall 5% overweight to oil, one finds an underweight of 5% in front-month WTI crude, an overweight of 5% in deferred Brent crude, and an overweight of 5% in Light Louisiana Sweet (LLS). The WTI and LLS legs offset each other with a possible view toward continued inventory

Risk View	Acct	Index	Factor	Look Thru
Commodity	XYZ	DJ-UBS	% Market Value	Yes

Sector/Maturity	0-3m	3m-6m	6m-1yr	1yr-2yr	2yr-3yr	3yr-5yr	5yr-10yr	10yr+	Total
Oil/Products	0.0%	5.0%	0.0%	0.0%	0.0%	0.0%	0.0%	0.0%	5.0%
Natural Gas	-3.0%	0.0%	3.0%	0.0%	0.0%	0.0%	0.0%	0.0%	0.0%
Industrial Metals	2.0%	0.0%	0.0%	0.0%	-2.0%	0.0%	0.0%	0.0%	0.0%
Precious Metals	0.0%	0.0%	-5.0%	0.0%	0.0%	0.0%	0.0%	0.0%	-5.0%
Grains	2.5%	0.0%	0.0%	0.0%	0.0%	0.0%	0.0%	0.0%	2.5%
Softs	-2.0%	0.0%	2.0%	0.0%	0.0%	0.0%	0.0%	0.0%	0.0%
Livestock	0.0%	0.0%	0.0%	0.0%	0.0%	0.0%	0.0%	0.0%	0.0%
Total	-0.5%	5.0%	0.0%	0.0%	-2.0%	0.0%	0.0%	0.0%	2.5%

Oil/Products	0-1m	1m-2m	2m-3m	3m-6m	6m-1yr	1yr-2yr	2yr-3yr	3yr-5yr	5yr-10yr	10yr+	Total
WTI Crude	-5.0%	0.0%	0.0%	0.0%	-2.0%	0.0%	2.5%	0.0%	0.0%	0.0%	-4.5%
Brent Crude	0.0%	0.0%	0.0%	5.0%	0.0%	0.0%	-2.5%	0.0%	0.0%	0.0%	2.5%
LLS Crude	0.0%	5.0%	0.0%	0.0%	0.0%	0.0%	0.0%	0.0%	0.0%	0.0%	5.0%
Heating Oil	0.0%	0.0%	2.0%	0.0%	0.0%	0.0%	0.0%	0.0%	0.0%	0.0%	2.0%
Gasoil	0.0%	0.0%	-2.0%	0.0%	0.0%	0.0%	0.0%	0.0%	0.0%	0.0%	-2.0%
Rbob Gasoline	0.0%	0.0%	0.0%	0.0%	0.0%	0.0%	0.0%	0.0%	0.0%	0.0%	0.0%
Gulf Coast Gasoline	0.0%	0.0%	0.0%	0.0%	2.0%	0.0%	0.0%	0.0%	0.0%	0.0%	2.0%
Total	-5.0%	5.0%	0.0%	5.0%	0.0%	0.0%	0.0%	0.0%	0.0%	0.0%	5.0%

Brent Crude	0-1m	1m-2m	2m-3m	3m-6m	6m-1yr	1yr-2yr	2yr-3yr	3yr-5yr	5yr-10yr	10yr+	Total
Physical	0.0%	0.0%	0.0%	0.0%	0.0%	0.0%	0.0%	0.0%	0.0%	0.0%	0.0%
Futures/Swaps	0.0%	0.0%	0.0%	5.0%	0.0%	0.0%	0.0%	0.0%	0.0%	0.0%	5.0%
Options	0.0%	0.0%	0.0%	0.0%	0.0%	0.0%	-2.5%	0.0%	0.0%	0.0%	-2.5%
Total	0.0%	0.0%	0.0%	5.0%	0.0%	0.0%	-2.5%	0.0%	0.0%	0.0%	2.5%

Exhibit 11-4 An Example of a Risk and Position Management System Built to Provide a Mix of an Intuitive High-Level View and a More Detailed and Granular View

Source: PIMCO. Sample for illustrative purposes only.

builds and decoupling of Cushing crude prices from other global benchmarks. The Brent crude position is an outright long oil position, perhaps expressing a view on increased geopolitical tensions developing in the Middle East. Further, one finds a 2% overweight in heating oil versus a 2% underweight in gas oil. Finally, in the two-year–three-year bucket, this representative account is 2% underweight Brent versus overweight WTI, expecting an eventual convergence between these two locations.

For the specialist portfolio manager, it is important to be able to drill down still further in order to see where the Brent exposure comes from, be it swaps, options, futures, or physical. As illustrated at the bottom of Exhibit 11-4, drilling into the Brent position, we find an outright long in the three-month–six-month bucket. In addition, we find that the 2.5% underweight in the two-year–three-year bucket is expressed through options (matched by an offsetting overweight in WTI options). And there is one final level: each of the individual securities themselves. In the case of a swap or ETF on a broad commodity index, some of these positions would be only implied, as they are embedded into a larger structure.

At every level, rather than view the positions in terms of deviations from the index by percent of market value, one can view them in terms of VaR or tracking error, using any of the four correlation matrices listed in the previous section.

COUNTERPARTY RISK MANAGEMENT

While managing and monitoring market risk is important, managing counterparty risk is equally important in a derivatives-based strategy. Investing in commodity indexes, whether via total return swaps or futures, involves derivatives-based exposures. While the counterparty risk of a futures transaction is limited in many respects by the presence of the exchange and the regular daily margining, it is still important to only deal with counterparties that have sound risk management practices and are in good financial standing.

MF Global's bankruptcy in 2011 and their practice of co-mingling segregated client funds with company funds is a prime example of the importance of dealing with reputable counterparties with sound risk management. Prior to MF Global, in 2005 Refco's bankruptcy resulted in the temporary freeze on client assets, and while money may not have been lost, it is another reminder of the potential problems that can still emerge.

In the case of OTC transactions involving derivatives, the need for stringent counterparty management is clear. If the counterparty to an OTC trade goes bankrupt, the investors lose the exposure that they had, and they must reinitiate that exposure with another counterparty. During the time the investor does not have exposure, the market may experience a material move in prices. Furthermore, the investors are also stuck in a long, drawn-out battle with other creditors in an attempt to collect any paper gains they had on the original derivatives transaction.

This is why derivative counterparties for all trades, including those where a futures exchange is involved, must be vetted and approved regularly by a designated risk committee. At PIMCO, there is a specific counterparty risk committee that oversees this process. This committee has representation from the senior levels of every business unit at PIMCO and works with PIMCO's credit analysts to take into account the financial capability as well as risk management practices of every potential counterparty (see Exhibit 11-5). The approved derivatives counterparty list is reviewed at least quarterly.

Counterparty risk can be further minimized by having good legal agreements and operational practices in place. For example, swap agreements should be written so that they are uniform and consistent across all counterparties and contain definitions of standard events of default or termination such as bankruptcy, failure to pay, credit events (ratings change), tax events, etc. In addition, the traders and portfolio managers should know the details of each trade executed. This goes beyond the pricing and economic terms. For example, suppose there is a gold variance swap that was traded and the reference price is the London p.m. gold fix price.

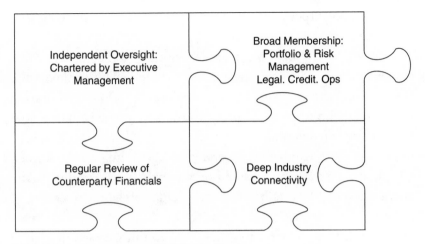

Exhibit 11-5 **Counterparty Risk Committee**

What are the procedures if no London p.m. fix was set but an a.m. fix was? Does it matter if the disruption was due to a holiday or a technical problem? What if any acceleration or termination triggers exist, and what exactly are the closeout procedures in the case of any of the termination clauses being triggered? What price is used if there was a limit move in a commodity on a given day? Thoroughly understanding the answers to these and other questions is essential when dealing with derivatives in order to prevent finding out at exactly the wrong time that there was some one-off exception to the general rules. These same questions need to be asked whether the counterparty is an investment bank or an exchange clearinghouse. Historically the risk of the clearinghouse has been considered minimal, but new legislation may lead to the creation of more clearinghouses without the history of the earlier established exchanges.

RISK MANAGEMENT FOR THE COLLATERAL PORTFOLIO

We now turn to best risk management practices on the collateral portfolio underlying the commodity exposure. This can be further separated into two aspects: the operational aspect, making sure margin exchange is seamless and error free, and the active management aspect, where one is taking positions in the fixed-income markets, attempting to outperform the three-month T-bill or other collateral benchmark, as the case may be.

Strong operational practices are another vital component of a complete approach to risk management. Being able to support the frequent and timely exchange of collateral for OTC positions is important in limiting counterparty exposure. There should be a close collaboration among traders, front-office staff, risk management, back office, and custodian banks. Several years ago, it might have seemed acceptable to exchange collateral on a weekly basis; but during the credit crisis of 2008, daily and even intraday exchange of collateral was essential, and that remains true today.

In addition to operations designed to mitigate counterparty risk, strong operational controls are essential in making sure that appropriate cash flows are made and received. OTC derivatives transactions often have relatively complicated payoff functions or reference some nonmarket observable asset such as a custom commodity index. It is the job of the calculation agent in the OTC transaction (typically the Wall Street bank that is the counterparty) to calculate the amount that the investor is to pay or to receive. However, it is entirely possible that mistakes can be made during this process. Therefore, it is essential that an investor be able to support independent verification of all index calculations and cash flows for derivatives transactions at maturity as well as on a daily mark-to-market basis. Beyond the concerns briefly highlighted above, there are further operational risk controls that must be in place when dealing with physical commodities.

As far as active management goes, part of it is the same prudent management as one would do for any fixed-income portfolio—understanding and managing duration, credit (sovereign, corporate, and individual in the case of asset-backed securities), convexity, and curve risk. Perhaps as important as these "standard" fixed-income risk factors is liquidity risk. If one allocates the entire collateral backing away from T-bills in an effort to enhance returns, how is one to meet the frequent and often large and persistent margin calls that commodity investing entails in a timely fashion?

MONITORING LIQUIDITY

PIMCO, for instance, uses a layered approach to liquidity. The portfolio is segmented into liquidity tiers: Tier 1 is essentially pure cash (accessible the same day, or T + 0); this tier includes T-bills and other Treasuries, STIF, time deposits, CD, and CP, as well as repurchase agreements. Tier 2 is accessible on a T + 3 basis with very low transaction costs; this tier consists of short-maturity A-rated and higher corporate bonds, non-USD government bonds, etc. Finally, Tier 3 represents the illiquid assets that could entail significant transaction costs to liquidate, especially in a stressed or falling market. Correlations of these securities with the financial conditions that could lead to strong commodity market sell-offs should be taken into consideration. The appropriate amount to hold in each tier is determined by a combination of quantitative modeling and the PIMCO Investment Committee's view of market conditions. Under normal circumstances, Tier 1 assets are a maximum of the two-day, 95% conditional VaR (maximum loss assuming the VaR limit has been breached) using either a variance-covariance matrix with data drawn from highly volatile periods (such as 1998–1999, 2000–2001, 2007–2008) or a custom stress scenario devised by the PIMCO Investment Committee. Also in normal circumstances, Tier 3 assets would be less than 50% of the portfolio.

CONCENTRATION RISK

Credit and concentration limits are also extremely important in the fixed-income collateral portfolio. As mentioned earlier in this chapter, in the 2007 and 2008 periods, a couple of commodity index funds managed by well-known investment firms were forced to close due to poor risk management of their collateral portfolios. One of them had essentially all of its collateral invested in a commodity-linked note issued by Lehman Brothers (poor credit research and management of concentration risk), while another had a substantial portion of its portfolio invested in subprime asset-backed securities that were highly rated by the ratings agencies but suffered significant principal losses anyway (poor credit research). These examples highlight the importance for investors to do thorough and independent credit analysis regardless of whether investing in sovereign government bonds, corporate bonds, or asset-backed securities. In addition, concentration limits should be imposed not just on the individual issuer but also by sector and even by country. This could protect against systematic debasement in entire sectors (financials, mortgages, etc.) or even countries (Greece, Portugal, etc.).

Finally, the best risk management tools and paradigm should seamlessly combine the risk from commodity positions with those from the collateral portfolio. Once this is in place, an intelligent commodity indexer has the ability to consistently add value, from multiple sources, over any commodity index.

We hope we have given you a comprehensive overview, with examples, of best practices in intelligent commodity indexing. We started with a history of commodity index investing and the origin of the most popular commodity indexes. We then moved on to discuss ways for an intelligent investor to outperform these indexes by exploiting inefficiencies and structural risk premiums both in the commodity markets and in the collateral pool underlying the commodity futures. We illustrated these with a number of examples. Finally, we moved on to a discussion of the actual implementation and subsequent risk management of these strategies.

All of the ideas discussed previously can be improved upon given greater fundamental knowledge about the different sectors of the commodity market. Knowledge about the fundamentals of each market can help an investor make more informed decisions when implementing structural trades, and it can help in identifying new structural trades. Greater knowledge of commodity fundamentals can also improve the risk management process by understanding what are the macro or micro risk factors that drive a given portfolio volatility. Given the benefits that a fundamental understanding can provide in intelligent commodity indexing, in the following chapter we present a brief overview of the major fundamental factors that are most important to each of the commodity sectors.

CHAPTER 12

Commodity Fundamentals

Preceding chapters have outlined multiple different structural opportunities available for the commodity index investor. These structural opportunities are the result of risk premiums embedded in either the term structure of commodity prices, the price of options, or the spread between the price of commodities of different locations or grades. However, fundamental developments in either commodity or outside markets can often cause commodity prices to move in such a way that the risk premium is overwhelmed and the expected profit from a structural trade turns into a loss. There are many examples of this happening, and sometimes it happens in a very large way. Some examples include the brutally cold winter of 1995 that sent the March–April natural gas spread to a 20% backwardation, the 2008 financial crisis that caused realized crude oil volatility to spike northward of 100%, and the 2011 backup of crude oil in the U.S. Midwest that caused WTI to trade to a $27 discount of Brent. In all these cases, knowledge of the underlying fundamentals in the various commodity markets would have allowed an investor to make better, more informed decisions.

Knowledge of the fundamentals in each market helps give the intelligent index investor an edge in several important ways. First, fundamental knowledge of various markets can provide a road map for finding structural opportunities. Second, it can enable an investor to understand what fundamental changes could occur that could cause the structural risk premium to not be realized or possibly result in losses on the trade. This can help an investor to better quantify the risks to a trade, look for correlations or concentrations to similar risk factors across multiple trades, and possibly look for hedges to offset some of these risks. Fundamental insights can also give an investor the confidence to bet against a recent trend and benefit from a reversion in long-run relationships. After all, the point when spreads between two substitutable commodities like wheat and corn reach their widest is often the hardest time to initiate a trade. Finally, the investor can better answer the question, "Is something different this time?"

Generally, structural commodity trades have a history of working well almost by definition. If they didn't work, they probably wouldn't have been identified as structural opportunities. In the case of oil, many index investors chose to hold length in Brent rather than WTI, as Brent had historically had a better roll yield. However, at some point things can change, as history need not always repeat itself. Certainly in the case of the spread between WTI and Brent crude oil, something was different in mid–2011. Prior to this, the spread had never traded wider than a few dollars; but in the third quarter of 2011, it widened out to $27. While this move worked in favor of those holding structural underweights to WTI, it doesn't always work out this way. Strong fundamental knowledge can allow investors to try and avoid some of these types of large market dislocations that are fundamental sea changes rather than structural dislocations. Given the importance of commodity fundamentals to the implementation and risk management of the ideas expressed in this book, in this chapter we will provide an overview of the fundamentals and key data releases that should be watched for each of the major commodity sectors.

ENERGY—OIL AND PRODUCTS

The supply side of the oil market is typically broken down at the highest level into production from the Organization of the Petroleum Exporting Countries (OPEC) and non-OPEC countries. Using data from the International Energy Agency (IEA) and PIMCO, Exhibit 12-1 shows the global production of crude oil at the country level broken down by OPEC member countries and non-OPEC countries. Within OPEC, the production of natural gas liquids is broken out separately.

OPEC member countries produce roughly 40% of the world's oil, with the remaining 60% coming from non-OPEC countries. However, even though non-OPEC producers contribute to the bulk of crude oil production, it is OPEC that will contribute most to the growth of future oil production in the coming years. Exhibit 12-2 shows the IEA's expectations for growth in the oil supply from 2010 to 2016.

One of the drivers for this is that many of the former sources of oil supply growth outside OPEC have peaked and are now in

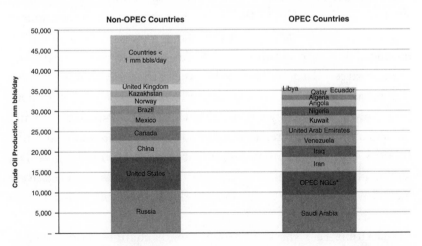

Exhibit 12-1 **Global Production of Crude Oil by OPEC Member Countries and Non-OPEC Countries**

* NGLs is natural gas liquids.

Source: International Energy Agency (IEA), PIMCO, as of February 15, 2012

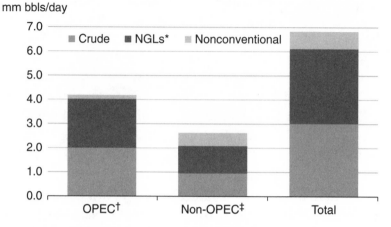

Exhibit 12-2 **Components of Global Oil Growth, 2010–2016**

* NGLs is natural gas liquids.

† OPEC crude is capacity additions.

‡ Global refinery processing gains included in non-OPEC.

Source: IEA, Medium-Term Oil and Gas Markets 2011

a state of flat to declining production. For example, the region of the Former Soviet Union (FSU) has been the single largest source of growth outside OPEC over the past 15 years. In 1995, the FSU produced just over 7 million barrels/day compared with nearly 13.5 million barrels/day in 2011. While some of this growth was attributable to tax reform and industry privatization, much of this production growth was merely a reversal of the decline in production and oil demand that occurred leading up to Russia's 1998 financial crisis. In 1988, Russia was producing at roughly 11 million barrels/day; and so adjusting for this, the production growth has been relatively muted over the past 20 years despite the fact that prices have more than quadrupled.

Exhibit 12-3 shows expectations for changes by country in non-OPEC crude supply over the next several years. As seen in the exhibit, countries such as Russia, Mexico, the United Kingdom, and Norway, sources of tremendous production growth over the past several decades, are all seeing steadily declining production.

mm bbls/day

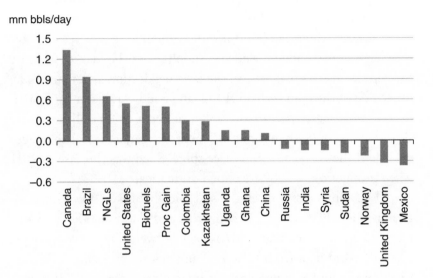

Exhibit 12-3 Non-OPEC Supply: Change, 2010–2016

* NGLs is natural gas liquids.

Source: IEA, Medium-Term Oil and Gas Markets 2011

These losses are offset by growth in the Americas, thanks to relatively new technologies that allow extraction of oil from new opportunities like oil sands, shale, and deep water. However, the lack of
growth or even outright decline in more mature producing regions
will weigh heavily on the ability of non-OPEC countries to produce
meaningful growth in the supply of oil.

OPEC producers are unique from non-OPEC producers
because they typically manage their crude oil production, both at
the country level and at the aggregate OPEC level, in order to balance the market and smooth changes in inventories and prices. At
the country level, it is essentially the core OPEC member countries,
which primarily consist of Saudi Arabia, Kuwait, and the United
Arab Emirates, that in practice do most of the production adjust-
ments. Non-OPEC countries, on the other hand, typically produce
at close to maximum capacity. Therefore, even though non-OPEC
producers supply the majority of the world's oil, the OPEC producers are the largest swing factor on the supply side in any given year.

The dynamic nature of OPEC means that there is some potential of a soft floor to the price of oil if OPEC member countries can collectively remove enough crude oil supply from the market in order to keep the market balanced in the face of a decline in demand. The other side of the coin is that OPEC, and Saudi Arabia in particular, is expected to have spare capacity that can be brought online to meet short-term supply disruptions and help mitigate physical shortages of oil and the corresponding price spike. Such was the case in 2011 when production in Libya declined dramatically.

The demand side of oil is also typically broken down into two groups, namely, the OECD countries and the non-OECD countries. There are two main differences between these two groups. First, demand data from OECD countries are available on a relatively timely and accurate basis. It is typically possible to disaggregate demand for OECD countries into how much of the demand for crude oil was for physical end use and how much was for changes in inventory levels. This type of detail is not possible in non-OECD countries, which provide little visibility on their overall crude oil inventory levels. The other difference between the OECD and non-OECD countries is that the OECD countries broadly have flat-to-declining oil demand growth, whereas non-OECD countries' oil demand is steadily growing. In aggregate, non-OECD oil demand now makes up close to 50% of global oil demand, and sometime in 2012 or 2013, it will likely be the majority of global oil demand, as illustrated in Exhibit 12-4. Given the lack of transparency and available data for non-OECD oil demand, this presents ever-increasing challenges for understanding the demand side of the equation in oil.

In terms of following the supply-demand balances in oil, the outlook for non-OECD and OECD demand plus non-OPEC and OPEC supply must be pieced together from various different sources. The most important and widely followed data for the oil market is by the Weekly Petroleum Status Report released every Wednesday by the U.S. Energy Information Administration (EIA). This report is important because the United States is the world's largest oil consumer by a wide margin, and changes in U.S. demand

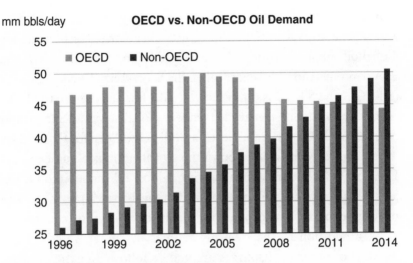

Exhibit 12-4 OECD Versus Non-OECD Oil Demand

Source: IEA, Medium-Term Oil and Gas Markets 2011

have a commensurate impact on the global oil balances. The weekly EIA report contains detailed data on U.S. demand by different product types such as gasoline, jet fuel, and distillate. It also has data on U.S. oil imports, production, and inventory levels. And in addition to the weekly data, the EIA produces a set of monthly data with the same level of detail. The monthly and weekly data do not necessarily always agree, as they are actually two distinct data sets, and so watching them both is often beneficial. The advantage of the weekly data is that they are timlier, given their higher frequency. However, the monthly data are often used to confirm the validity of the weekly data, given that the monthly data are generally more accurate and provide a truer picture of the state of oil supply and demand in the United States.

After the weekly EIA data, the next most watched set of data comes from the IEA's monthly Oil Market Report. The IEA's Oil Market Report is typically released around the twelfth of each month, and it represents an aggregation of the data that are submitted by individual countries. The IEA report is so widely watched because much of the underlying data are not made public except through this report.

This is why the IEA is the official source of oil data for the OECD and is generally taken to be the industry benchmark or baseline for global oil supply-demand balances. In addition to the IEA data, the EIA puts out a monthly report called the Short-Term Energy Outlook (STEO). The STEO is typically released a few days before the IEA's report. It contains estimates for current global supply, demand, and changes in OECD inventory levels as well as a forecast for these values over the next year. In addition to the global aggregate numbers, the EIA's STEO contains a breakdown of global oil supply into OPEC and the larger non-OPEC producers. On the demand side, the STEO provides country-level demand for the major consuming countries.

In addition to the monthly reports by the IEA and EIA, a handful of other data sources are widely followed in the oil market. In particular, China releases monthly production and trade data that contain data on oil imports and exports and refinery production. These data are frequently the basis for estimates of Chinese oil demand; this information is quite important considering that China is the world's second largest oil consumer and data on China's consumption are relatively limited. In addition to Chinese oil trade data, inventory data from Japan, Singapore, and Europe are closely watched. Singapore's oil inventory report is released by International Enterprise and is important given Singapore's status as a regional oil trading hub. The level of Japanese stocks is also released weekly from the Petroleum Association of Japan. The importance of Japanese stocks has diminished over the years as a result of Japan's structurally declining crude oil demand; however, the report remains important since it is one of the few high-frequency, weekly sources for the level of crude inventories in Asia. Insight into European inventories can be achieved by looking at weekly reports from PJK International covering the Amsterdam-Rotterdam-Antwerp (ARA) area. ARA is Europe's oil trading hub, and the weekly inventory report provides insights into the level of crude inventories in Europe.

Finally, the Joint Organizations Data Initiative (JODI) is a relatively newer source of oil market data that are a corroboration between producer and consumer countries. The data from JODI are provided by individual countries, and this information is growing in importance as the quality of the data improves and becomes more standardized. The JODI data cover both oil and products, including demand, supply, and inventories for more than 90 participating countries. The drawback of the JODI data is that they are only available after a lag of one to two months, they are often revised, and the data are often inconsistent with other data sources. However, JODI data are generally the market standard for information on Saudi Arabian production and demand.

The above discussion of fundamentals focused on oil-specific data releases. However, there are also other fundamental data that should be watched. One example is macro indicators that have a strong correlation to overall economic activity and GDP. This is important as there is a high correlation between economic growth and increases in oil demand. This relationship is depicted in Exhibit 12-5, which shows the year-over-year growth in oil demand along with the year-over-year growth in global GDP. Given this tight relationship, macro indicators such as GDP and

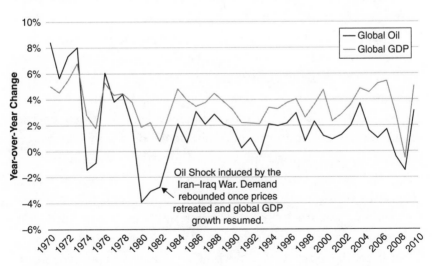

Exhibit 12-5   The Primary Driver of Oil Demand Growth Is Global GDP

Source: Bloomberg, IEA, as of June 30, 2011

industrial production for the major oil-consuming countries like the United States, China, and Japan are influential factors for the oil market.

Finally, the geopolitical state of the world and high-level geopolitical risks constitute another factor that, while hard to quantify, clearly must be factored into any fundamental assessment of the global oil supply-demand balance. There is no single data release by which this last factor can be monitored, but it is a necessary part of following fundamentals in the oil market.

Exhibit 12-6 summarizes some of the key sources of fundamental information that are particularly relevant to the oil market.

ENERGY—NATURAL GAS

The U.S. natural gas market is different from oil in that it is much more U.S.-centric, and for the most part, it is a relatively closed system. Whereas in oil the majority of the crude supply comes from imports from a whole host of different countries, in natural gas close to 90% of the supply comes from domestic production. The balance of natural gas supply comes via pipeline from Canada and from liquefied natural gas imports. This means that for natural gas essentially all the basic fundamental supply, demand, and inventory information can be obtained from the EIA.

On the demand side, there are five major components that make up natural gas demand, and their relative importance is shown in Exhibit 12-7. Residential and commercial demand, which together represent roughly one-third of total demand, is primarily related to heating and cooling applications. Industrial demand represents slightly less than one-third of total demand and is used in various capacities across many different industries. For example, natural gas is used as a feedstock for many different chemicals and products, ranging from fertilizers to plastics. Many industries also use it as an energy source for processes like powering boilers to produce steam. The largest source of natural gas demand is for electric power generation. While coal-powered plants produce most of the electricity

Data Release	Summary of Information	Timing
EIA Petroleum Status Report	Comprehensive data on U.S. production, demand, imports, inventories, etc.	Weekly, Wednesday
IEA Oil Market Report	Industry baseline for global oil supply and demand, broken down by country.	Monthly, around the 12th
EIA Short-Term Energy Outlook	High-level view of global supply, demand, and OECD inventories.	Monthly, between the 6th and 12th
Chinese Monthly Production & Trade Data	Refinery runs and oil imports-exports	Monthly, midmonth
Singapore Oil Inventory Report	Inventories held by industry in Singapore, Asia's oil trading hub	Weekly, Thursday
Japan Oil Inventory Report	Inventories held by industry in Japan	Weekly, Wednesday
ARA Oil Inventory Report	Inventories held by industry in the ARA area, Europe's oil trading hub	Weekly, Thursday
JODI Database	High-level view of global supply, demand, and inventories	Monthly

Exhibit 12-6 **Key Sources of Information on the Oil Market**

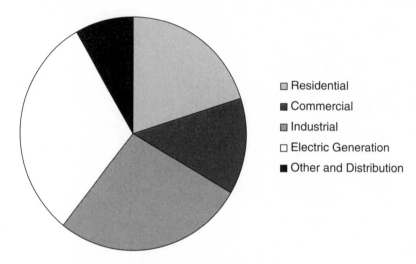

Exhibit 12-7 Natural Gas Demand by Sector

Source: EIA, as of December 31, 2011

in the United States, natural gas plants are growing in use, given increasing environmental regulations combined with their competitive relative costs and increased operational flexibility. Finally, the "other" category in Exhibit 12-7 is just the gas needed to run the whole system (distribution, pipeline operation, etc).

Considering the sources of natural gas demand, it is not surprising that natural gas demand is highly seasonal. Natural gas demand tends to be highest in the winter months and much lower during the spring through fall. This basic seasonal dynamic is driven by residential and commercial heating demand, which tends to peak during the winter months. In addition, recent years have seen an increasing amount of natural gas demand coming from power generation as older coal and nuclear plants are replaced by gas-fired power plants. This has resulted in a new seasonal dynamic during the hottest summer months. During the hottest part of summer when air-conditioning demand peaks, there is increasingly an uptick in natural gas demand, since much of the electricity that is produced to meet this demand comes from gas-fired plants. Exhibit 12-8 shows this typical seasonal pattern for natural gas demand.

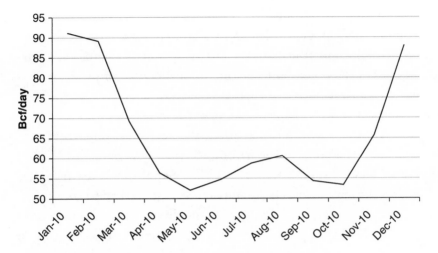

Exhibit 12-8   Average Daily Natural Gas Demand in 2010

Source: EIA, As of December 31, 2011

Weather is generally the most important fundamental factor in the natural gas market, since residential and commercial demand plus electricity generation and even some industrial demand are all tied to heating and cooling needs. Daily weather updates and forecasts can be obtained from the National Oceanic and Atmospheric Administration's (NOAA) National Weather Service. However, the private or subscription-based services and data provided by companies like EarthSat are generally the most widely followed within the market. These companies take the underlying weather forecasts from sources such as NOAA and convert them into a more useful form, such as population-weighted cooling degree or heating degree days. These measures reflect the demand for energy needed to heat or cool a building, and as such, they are more useful inputs for forecasting demand for natural gas.

In addition to weather forecasts and their implications for heating and cooling demand, major weather events such as hurricanes must be monitored. There is sizable domestic natural gas production that is situated in and around the Gulf of Mexico, although the importance of this production has declined since the early 2000s.

In addition to the production resources around the Gulf of Mexico, a substantial amount of demand is also tied to this region through residential, commercial, and industrial demand. Therefore, a hurricane has the potential to disrupt large amounts of production as well as demand. Such a disruption could have a large impact on both spot prices and the shape of the forward curve.

After changes in the weather, the next most important fundamental data point in the natural gas market is the EIA's Weekly Natural Gas Storage Report. While changes in inventories are important across most commodity markets since they provide information about the relative balance of supply and demand, inventories are particularly important in natural gas due to the seasonality in demand and constraints on the amount of storage available.

As previously discussed, natural gas demand is highly seasonal and peaks in the winter, but natural gas supply is relatively constant throughout the year. During the spring through fall months when the market is oversupplied, natural gas is injected into storage. This gas will then be withdrawn from storage during the winter to meet the higher levels of demand. If inventories either prior to or during the winter are too low, then price must be used to ration those inventories and make them last for the entire winter. Similarly, if inventories are too high prior to the time when inventories start to draw, then they could exceed the capacity of storage, which would require pushing prices so low that additional demand is brought forward or supply is shut in at the wellhead. The level of natural gas inventories is so important because there is a band of acceptable levels for starting the winter and ending the winter, and prices must constantly adjust to try and manage that process.

The remainder of the natural gas–specific fundamental information is largely related to supply. On a daily basis, it is possible to get the actual volume of physical gas that flows through a given point on all the major pipelines in the United States. Bentek is one company that processes all this natural gas flow data (referred to as pipeline nomination data), aggregates the data, and provides the information on a fee basis to market participants.

In addition to pipeline nomination data, there are other publicly available, albeit less timely, sources of natural gas supply information. The EIA puts out its Monthly Natural Gas Gross Production Report, sometimes referred to as the "914 report," which provides detailed data on natural gas production. In addition, the EIA's STEO, discussed in the oil section, includes natural gas supply-demand balances. Baker Hughes and Smith Bits both put out data on rig counts each Friday that can be used to determine production rates and drilling activity. On top of this, many industry participants watch the quarterly and annual filings released by exploration and production companies for insights into projections on future spending for natural gas drilling and exploration.

Finally, if considering the outlook for natural gas over a longer time horizon, then regulatory updates from the Environmental Protection Agency and the Federal Energy Regulatory Commission must be monitored. Regulation could have a substantial impact on both the supply side and demand side for natural gas. The growth in supply from shale gas, along with the environmental regulation of these processes, is one source of uncertainty. On the demand side, the possibility for regulation of carbon emissions and a growing emphasis on clean energy are two issues that must be monitored.

Exhibit 12-9 summarizes some of the key sources of fundamental information that are particularly relevant to the natural gas market.

AGRICULTURE—GRAINS

The United States is the world's largest grain producer and the world's largest grain exporter by a significant margin. The country is the single biggest factor in the global supply-demand balances and is key in determining the global prices of various grains. Because of the United States' large share of the global agricultural market and agriculture's importance to the U.S. economy, there is an abundance of quality fundamental data that are updated frequently for the grain markets. These data, largely published by different groups within

Data Release	Summary of Information	Timing
Weather Updates	Weather is the key swing factor for demand	Daily and intraday
EIA Weekly Natural Gas Storage Report	Amount of natural gas in storage	Weekly, Thursday
Pipeline Nomination Data	Gas volumes flowing through major pipelines	Daily
914 Report	Production data across the United States	Monthly
EIA Short-Term Energy Outlook	High-level view of supply and demand	Monthly, between the 6th and 12th
Rig Counts	Data on drilling activity and production rates	Weekly, Friday

Exhibit 12-9 Key Sources of Information on the Natural Gas Market

the U.S. Department of Agriculture (USDA), cover everything from U.S. production and inventory levels to global supply-demand balances by country. (*Note:* In this chapter, while soybeans are not actually a grain, we use the convention common in the commodity index world of grains to include corn, soybeans, and wheat.)

In terms of monitoring the fundamentals for the grain markets, typically the supply side of the market is the most important. This is because the supply side is significantly more uncertain and has a higher volatility from year to year than the demand side. As an example of this supply-side volatility, Exhibit 12-10 shows the year-over-year change in global production and global consumption for corn for the past 20 years. Over the period from 1988 to 2011, the volatility of the yearly change in global corn consumption was just 2.3%, compared with a volatility of 7.7% for the yearly change in corn production. The changes in consumption are relatively small and are primarily in response to changes in the price of corn, which generally is a result of changes in the level of production. The same phenomenon of changes in production being more volatile and driving changes in prices and ultimately changes in demand is observed in the other grain and agricultural markets too.

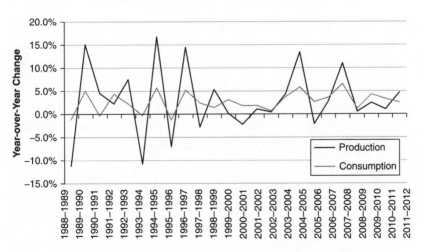

Exhibit 12-10 **Year-over-Year Change in Global Corn Supply and Demand**

Source: USDA, as of December 31, 2011

Given the supply and demand dynamics in grains, it makes most sense to start a fundamental analysis of the grain markets by analyzing the supply side of the market. The principal U.S. growing regions for the major grain crops are shown in Exhibit 12-11. What is interesting to note is just how concentrated the bulk of production is. The United States produces nearly 40% of the world's corn, and just six states are responsible for nearly 70% of that production.

The supply side is basically determined by two factors. The first is the amount of acreage that is planted, and the second is the yield of those acres. The amount of acreage planted to each crop is a function of the total amount of acres planted and also the distribution of those acres to each crop. When grain prices are high, then the overall amount of acreage will likely increase as more marginal, lower-yielding acres are brought into production. The relative mix between acres of different crops is a function of the crop rotation patterns that farmers follow combined with the relative prices of different grains.

Essentially farmers' decisions are made to maximize profits, and if the profit per acre will be highest for planting corn in a given year, then the total number of acres planted to corn will likely increase. The weather can also impact plantings, as different crops each have certain windows of time where they can be planted. If planted outside that window, then yields are often reduced, and crops are more sensitive to adverse weather. For example, excessive rain may result in an inability to complete needed field work prior to corn planting, causing a rotation into soybeans that can be planted later in the season. Such weather or other external events can force farmers to consider planting crops other than what simple economics might suggest.

In terms of data about plantings in the United States, the USDA releases estimates for the acreage to be planted for a host of crops at the end of March in its Prospective Plantings report. The data in the Prospective Plantings report are generally the first official estimate of acreage for the upcoming year's crops; the information is obtained by surveying tens of thousands of farm operators across the country. The report covers the major crops of corn, soybeans, and

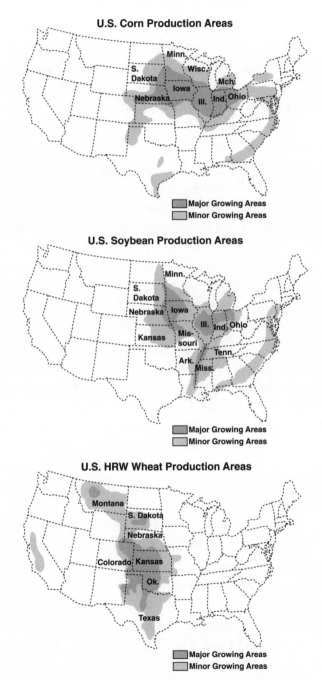

Exhibit 12-11 Growing Regions for the Major Grain Crops in the United States

Source: NOAA/USDA

wheat, as well as more minor crops like canola and rice. (As an aside, the USDA has an annual estimate of plantings for many crops such as corn and soybeans in its February Outlook, which can give some insights about planting decisions prior to the Prospective Plantings report. Also, the data on winter wheat acreage are first available in early January via the Winter Wheat Seedings report.) The next major data point for determining U.S. crop acreage is the Acreage report released at the end of June. The Acreage report is very similar to the Prospective Plantings report, but given that it occurs after most of the crop has been planted, it is much more accurate.

The second factor affecting supply is yields. The yield for a given crop is primarily driven by the time of planting and the weather following planting. The most important weather factors are temperature and precipitation, but the yield is ultimately a complex interaction among many different variables including factors such as the amount of nitrogen in the soil, the level of soil moisture, and the presence of various weeds or pesticides. How all these fundamental factors interact affects the condition of the crop and ultimately the yield. The condition of the crop can be monitored on a weekly basis through the USDA's weekly Crop Progress report. The Crop Progress report is released each Monday during the growing season, and the condition of the various crops is rated on a five-point scale ranging from excellent to very poor. While the correlation between crop condition and final yields can vary significantly, it is an important weekly data point.

Actual yield projections for U.S. crops can be obtained from the monthly World Agricultural Supply and Demand Estimates (WASDE) report. In addition to data on yields, the WASDE report also contains full supply-demand balances for the United States as well as high-level global balances. The WASDE report is typically released around the tenth of each month, and it is generally the industry baseline in terms of building both U.S. and global supply-demand balances. While the USDA typically sets the baseline for the industry, there are numerous private companies that try and improve upon the work the USDA does. The larger of these companies, such as Informa, typically release data like acreage and production estimates on a slightly earlier schedule than the USDA. Since these companies' data releases are well followed, it is not uncommon for their announcements to be market-moving events.

On the demand side, the WASDE provides the baseline for the market on a monthly basis. The WASDE gives a breakdown of U.S. demand by major categories. For example, in corn, this includes demand from feed, food, ethanol, and exports. While the WASDE provides monthly updates, there are many other reports that give insights into these major demand areas on a more frequent basis.

The most important of these other reports are the Export Sales released by the USDA each Thursday and, to a lesser extent, the U.S. ethanol production data released by the EIA each Wednesday. The export sales data are important because they are a high-frequency indication of the pace of exports relative to market expectations. For example, if export sales are low week after week, then often the USDA may revise down its estimate of export sales for the year. Similarly, the EIA's ethanol production data serve as a high-frequency check against the market's expectations on the pace of ethanol production. Other reports, such as U.S. crush data for soybeans or Cattle on Feed reports, are also sources of high-frequency demand indications, but they generally have smaller market impact.

The above reports and discussion focused on explicit supply and demand information. However, the USDA also issues a Grain Stocks report on a quarterly basis. The Grain Stocks report is possibly the most important in terms of market impact of all the reports released by the USDA. It contains a comprehensive measure of the actual amount of inventory of grain held in the United States. Given that there is a restocking of inventory only once per year, at harvest, the changes in inventories outside the harvest period are actually a very direct measure of demand. This is what makes the Grain Stocks report so important. It doesn't just tell the market how much of an inventory buffer is available to absorb future production shortfalls; it actually is a very direct measure of the pace of demand. Given this, the Grain Stocks report is almost a process of marking to market the assumptions that the market has made with respect to actual physical demand for grain. This means the report can have very large market impacts since it can cause the market to reassess prior assumptions on the level of demand. And after harvest, the report can help to provide additional certainty about the size of the crop.

The above discussion of fundamental analysis and data focused largely on the United States. While the United States is the most watched country because of the abundance of high-quality data and the fact that it is the world's largest corn and soybean producer and the fourth largest wheat producer, it is also important to monitor crop development in the other major producing and exporting countries. In corn, the most important countries to monitor are the United States, Brazil, and Argentina, as together they account for roughly 50% of global production and 75% of global exports. In soybeans, these same countries account for roughly 80% of global production and 85% of global exports. In wheat, it is the large exporters that are the most important to monitor, as production is relatively globally distributed and often based on domestic demand. The United States is the world's largest wheat exporter, with nearly 20% market share, followed by the EU, Canada, Russia, and Australia, which each represents around 10 to 15% of global exports.

For all major producing countries highlighted above, the monthly WASDE provides the most easily accessible, high-level expectations for domestic production and exports. For a more thorough analysis, the USDA's Foreign Agricultural Service (FAS) provides periodic Attaché Reports, which contain a summary and analysis of supply and demand changes for key importing and exporting countries. These reports can often be precursors to changes in the monthly WASDE reports. In addition, data from the local domestic equivalents of the USDA can be monitored. For example, in Brazil, CONAB puts out periodic updates on crop expectations during the growing season; and in Argentina, Bolsa de Cereales puts out weekly updates. Finally, the most real-time, yet noisiest, data relate to the weather in key growing regions around the world. While the weather's ultimate impact on production is often difficult to assess because of the interplay among temperature, precipitation, soil moisture, etc., it is most often the underlying cause for changes that later show up in different official supply estimates.

Exhibit 12-12 summarizes some of the key sources of fundamental information that are particularly relevant to the grain markets.

AGRICULTURE—SOFTS

The term *softs* traditionally refers to commodities that are grown rather than mined. However, within the index space, the grain markets (corn, wheat, and soybeans) are usually treated separately, leaving softs to represent the nongrain agricultural commodities such as sugar, cotton, coffee, and cocoa. In terms of analysis, the softs are quite similar to the grains. Demand is relatively stable, and it is production surprises that typically introduce most of the fundamental volatility. After the production surprises occur, it is the sensitivity of demand to changes in price that drives future price changes.

For the cotton market, the largest producers are China, India, and the United States, accounting for nearly two-thirds of global production. The United States is the world's largest cotton exporter by a wide margin, and the United States and India together represent nearly 50% of global exports. The WASDE report, which contains estimates of U.S. and global cotton supply-demand balances, provides generally the most important data releases in the cotton market. The USDA's reports on weekly export sales and crop condition, which were discussed in the grains section, both cover the cotton market.

In addition to these reports that overlap with the grain market, there are also a few cotton-specific reports that are more narrowly followed but still important to those following the cotton market closely. The most important of these reports is probably the Cotton on Call report released each week by the Commodity Futures

Data Release	Summary of Information	Timing
WASDE	USDA's estimates for U.S. and global crop production and demand numbers	Monthly
Grain Stocks	Quarter-end inventory levels for major U.S. crops, implied demand	Quarterly
Acreage	Planted acreage for major U.S. crops	Annual, end of June
Prospective Plantings	Survey of farmers' planting intentions for the coming year	Annual, end of March
Export Sales	U.S. grain sales to foreign countries	Weekly, Thursday
U.S. Ethanol Production	Weekly ethanol production	Weekly, Wednesday
Crop Progress	Crop condition and planting progress by state	Weekly, Monday
Weather Updates	Weather updates for key producing countries	Daily

Exhibit 12-12 Key Sources of Information on the Grain Markets

Trading Commission (CFTC). This report details the amount of cotton that has been contracted for sale but for which a price has not yet been fixed. Due to the way the cotton market works, sales at a given geographic location are often agreed to at a fixed spread to the futures contract. These sales show up in the Cotton on Call report. Therefore, the Cotton on Call report is watched to assess the amount of physical buying or selling that is taking place in the cotton market at a given price level.

The largest sources of supply in the sugar market are Brazil, India, and the EU, which in total produce roughly 50% of the world's sugar supply. The United States is the world's fifth largest sugar producer, and data about U.S. production is available in the USDA's WASDE report. In addition, the USDA maintains global sugar supply and demand data through the FAS. UNICA, the Brazilian Sugarcane Industry Association, releases data about production on a biweekly basis for the Center-South region of Brazil. Production data on this region of Brazil are watched closely since they represent the largest sugar-producing region in the world. Besides data from UNICA and the USDA, there is little official information that is closely watched by the market. Most of the important fundamental data come from private, consultant-type sources like Kingsman or F.O. Licht.

In terms of the other softs such as coffee and cocoa, there is no accepted authority for baseline market data. Just as it does for sugar, the USDA's FAS maintains data on global supply-demand balances on coffee, and it issues periodic reports updating global supply and demand information across key producing countries. The USDA data provide an accurate look at historic demand, but the information is useful more as a reference and not a source of new market data. Most of the fundamental information in these smaller soft commodity markets comes from private consultant-type services like F.O. Licht and others.

Exhibit 12-13 summarizes some of the key sources of public fundamental information that are particularly relevant to the softs markets.

Data Release	Summary of Information	Timing
WASDE	USDA's estimates for U.S. and global crop production and demand numbers	Monthly
Acreage	Planted acreage for major U.S. crops	Annual, end of June
Prospective Plantings	Survey of farmers' planting intentions for the coming year	Annual, end of March
Export Sales	U.S. grain sales to foreign countries	Weekly, Thursday
Crop Progress	Crop condition and planting progress by state	Weekly, Monday
Cotton on Call	Quantity of physical cotton bought or sold but with a price yet to be fixed	Weekly, Thursday
Center-South Brazil Production	Production estimates for largest sugar-producing region	Biweekly

Exhibit 12-13 **Key Sources of Information on the Softs Markets**

METALS—BASE METALS

In terms of fundamentals, the base metals markets are much more opaque than either the oil or grain markets. Fundamental data regarding the level of current production or consumption for key regions are not publicly available in a timely manner. There are trade groups for most of the different nonferrous metals that serve as collection points for much of the supply and demand data globally, but the data are often not particularly current. For example, the International Copper Study Group (ICSG) has a press release around the twentieth of each month that gives a high-level overview of global supply and demand trends and year-on-year growth rates. However, the ICSG data released in the December press release will only cover supply and demand data up through September. Industry groups like the ICSG are an excellent source of data on longer-term supply and demand trends and industry background, but they tend to not release data that give rise to large market reactions. As in most commodity markets, and particularly those without centralized sources of credible baseline market balances, more timely fundamental data can be obtained from private subscription services.

China is incredibly important to the base metals markets because it is both the largest consumer and the largest source of incremental demand growth for most industrial metals. For example, China represents 39% of global refined copper demand, 40% of global aluminum demand, and 44% of global lead demand. While China's impact is large today, it is becoming even more important going forward. In terms of incremental demand growth, China represented roughly 80% of demand growth for copper in 2010. Given China's importance, its import-export data are watched very closely. Preliminary import and export data are released around the tenth of each month, with final data typically released around the twentieth. China also releases nonferrous metal production data around the middle of each month. These data series can help to provide a somewhat current insight into Chinese metal demand. However, given the basis between Shanghai traded metal prices and global prices on the LME, and its impact on metal shipments, these data can be relatively noisy from month to month.

Given the combination of limited transparency and lagged supply and demand data, the base metals markets tends to closely watch macro fundamental data that are highly correlated to base metals demand. Examples include the Purchasing Managers' Index (PMI) and industrial production data both globally and for the larger global economies such as the United States, China, the Eurozone, and Japan. Several China-specific macro numbers are also watched quite closely, given China's dominant size in the base metals market. Chinese data on loan growth and the breakdown and changes in fixed-asset investment are particularly important.

Inventory levels are also closely watched by the market. The level of inventories is important to understanding how much of a buffer exists to absorb supply or demand shocks, and the changes in inventory levels can give insights into tightening or loosening supply-demand balances. The LME releases daily inventory data for all the base metals stocks held by exchange-approved warehouses. In addition to the LME, the Shanghai Futures Exchange releases weekly data for copper, zinc, and aluminum inventories, and COMEX also releases daily copper inventories. However, conclusions drawn from exchange-published inventory data should be taken with a grain of salt, as shell games are frequently played by large commercial players. It is common for large commercial participants to move metal out of LME warehouses into off-exchange warehouses, only to move the metal back into the LME warehouses at a later date. Despite this drawback, changes in exchange inventory levels are closely watched by market participants. In addition to exchange inventories, the inventory levels of consumers, producers, and merchants are important data points.

Exhibit 12-14 summarizes some of the key sources of fundamental information that are particularly relevant to the base metals market.

Data Release	Summary of Information	Timing
Global PMI and IP Data	Levels of aggregate demand and industrial activity	Monthly
Chinese Macro Data	Growth in Chinese new loans and fixed-asset investment	Monthly
Inventory Levels	Exchange and commercial inventory levels	Daily–monthly

Exhibit 12-14 Key Sources of Information on the Base Metals Market

METALS—PRECIOUS METALS

Gold is different from other commodities because it doesn't trade based upon supply and demand fundamentals in the same way as other commodities. Gold is unique because it is not consumed. Virtually all the gold that has been produced historically still exists today. Given this, the total supply of gold is not just a function of the amount of gold that gets mined each year; it is also a function of the scrap supply that comes from the existing stock of gold. By way of reference, the total stock of gold outstanding is estimated to be around 155,000 tons, while annual new mine production is around 2,600 tons. Of this stock, only a small part reenters the supply chain as scrap, but it is a much bigger swing factor in balancing the market than gold mine production. Exhibit 12-15 shows the amount of gold supplied from mine production and the amount supplied from scrap over the past 20 years. Notice that mine production is relatively stable, but scrap production is not. Scrap production changes dramatically over time. This dynamic means that gold mine production isn't as important a fundamental data point as new production data are for other commodities, and this is why gold is unique from a fundamental analysis perspective.

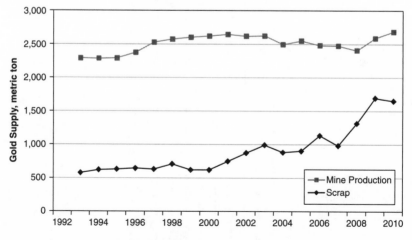

Exhibit 12-15 **Sources of Gold Supply**

Source: Bloomberg, Gold Fields Mineral Services, as of June 20, 2011

Since gold is not actually consumed, the total amount of supply and demand must match each year by definition. When demand exceeds the natural rate of scrap supply plus new mine production, additional scrap supply must be sourced. This additional supply is sourced via higher prices. As gold prices rise, the amount of scrap rises. Given this dynamic, understanding what drives demand for gold is particularly important. Gold demand is primarily used for jewelry and investment, which together account for around 80% of total demand. The remaining 20% comes from miscellaneous other sources like electronics, dental, and industrial demand. Jewelry demand is price sensitive and is fairly price elastic, falling as gold prices rise. Investment demand is driven largely by the desire to hold gold as a store of value or as an inflation hedge. The cost of that inflation hedge is measured by the level of real interest rates in an economy, i.e., the return that an investor forgoes by holding gold instead of some interest-bearing asset. If real interest rates are low, then demand for gold for investment will increase since the opportunity cost of holding gold is reduced. Similarly, high levels of real interest rates will reduce demand for gold. In particular, the level of real interest rates is the most important factor in influencing demand in the world's major gold-consuming countries—countries such as the United States, China, India, and Japan. To the extent that real rates tend to be inversely correlated with inflation, higher levels of inflation often equate to higher investment demand for gold.

Direct measurement for the level of investment demand can be observed from several different sources. First, the various gold ETFs report both their holdings of gold and the number of shares outstanding on a daily basis. In addition, the total amount of speculative length in gold futures is reported each Friday by the CFTC in its Commitment of Traders report. Finally, central banks have moved from net sellers of gold to net buyers of gold over the past decade, as emerging market central banks seek to diversify some of their U.S. dollar holdings. Central banks are the largest holders of gold globally, and their gold holdings are reported by the IMF on a lagged basis. However, even though the data about central bank gold buying are only often known long after the fact, they still can have large market impacts.

The rest of the precious metals complex tends to behave almost as a hybrid between gold and the base metals complex. Metals such as silver and platinum are influenced by the value of gold, as they too have similar store-of-value and inflation-hedging properties. However, silver and platinum also have many industrial uses. For example, in the case of platinum, auto catalyst and industrial demand represents close to 50% of all demand, with jewelry representing another 40% and investment only 10% of demand. Therefore, the precious metals aside from gold tend to trade with a beta to gold, but they will outperform or underperform depending on their own individual supply-demand balances. Just as in the case of base metals, indicators of industrial demand, such as global PMI and industrial production, are frequently watched closely by the market. Given the large share of demand for platinum from the automobile sector, the level of auto sales in the United States and Europe is also watched closely.

Exhibit 12-16 summarizes some of the key sources of fundamental information that are particularly relevant to the precious metals market.

CONCLUSION

In this chapter, we have outlined the major supply and demand drivers at work across the different commodity markets. We have also listed many of the important data releases that are watched closely by the market. Using this information, it is possible for index investors to stay abreast of major fundamental developments across the commodity sector. Tracking the fundamental data will help in understanding whether commodity price movements are driven by supply or demand changes. It will also allow for more informed decisions regarding structural commodity trades. It will aid investors in understanding if a given structural relationship is likely to be different this time and what factors could change that would make a given structural relationship no longer hold. Ultimately, the goal is that the knowledge of the fundamentals discussed in this chapter, while not exhaustive, will be a starting point to improve the trading and risk management of structural index positions.

Data Release	Summary of Information	Timing
Real Interest Rates/Inflation Levels	After-inflation returns on capital	Daily
ETF Holdings	Amount of money invested in gold ETFs	Daily
Central Bank Holdings	Central bank gold holdings	Monthly
Global PMI and IP Data	Levels of aggregate demand and industrial activity	Monthly
CFTC COT Report	Amount of speculative money invested in gold	Weekly, Friday

Exhibit 12-16 Key Sources of Information on the Precious Metals Market

CHAPTER 13

Index Development— The Next Phase

What are the properties that an ideal commodity index should possess? In our opinion, it must serve as a representation of the entire asset class, meaning it is well diversified across the various commodity sectors and has inflation-hedging properties, while offering better and more consistent long-term returns than the standard commodity indexes of today. A plethora of indexes are available today with back-tested histories that outperform the benchmark S&P GSCI and DJUBSCI. What the vast majority of these so-called second- and third-generation commodity indexes focuses on are variations on the basic characteristics of an index discussed in Chapter 1. These characteristics include positioning on the curve, choice of roll dates, and a rule (liquidity, world production, etc.) for choosing the weights. All of them choose to invest the collateral in three-month T-bills. However, the total return of a commodity index is a function of both the excess return on commodity futures and the return on collateral; hence choice of collateral is important as well. In this chapter, we outline some of the alternative indexes that have been constructed to date. As none of these fully incorporate many of the structural features discussed in this book, we conclude with an example of what a future index may look like.

CURVE POSITIONING

The most widely employed method of enhancing commodity index returns has so far focused on extending the tenor of the futures contracts that are held; therefore, we spend some time discussing this here (additional details on shifted indexes can be found in Chapter 7, "Calendar Spreads and Seasonal Strategies"). As an example, let's consider the DJUBS shifted indexes since they are the simplest, most common curve-based index enhancement. As such, the DJUBS shifted indexes should be thought of as the benchmark when assessing the real value added of any more complicated or dynamic curve-positioning strategies. The curve-positioning benefit of holding a broad basket of contracts further out the curve can be isolated by just comparing the DJUBS shifted index with the standard DJUBSCI. There are shifted indexes publicly published by Dow Jones all the way from one to five months out the curve, with additional tenors likely to be published in the future. (As a historical footnote, the original DJUBSCI could be thought of as a partially one-month shifted version of the S&P GSCI, with different weights.)

Shifted indexes became popular as investors responded to an increasing level of contango at the very front of the futures curve across several commodity markets. Since being introduced in July 2006, the various DJUBS shifted indexes have regularly outperformed the standard DJUBSCI by reducing the negative roll yield. The performance of the DJUBS two-month shifted index relative to the standard DJUBSCI is shown in Exhibit 13-1.

A portion of the improved roll yield and outperformance realized from holding contracts further out the curve is related to an increased risk premium further out the curve, as more distant contracts benefit from greater producer participation. Another source of outperformance in recent years has been avoiding some of the pressures related to the index roll in the front of the curve.

To the extent that commodity indexes impact the relative prices between contracts, they do so by decreasing the available risk premium. To avoid continued reduction in the risk premium that

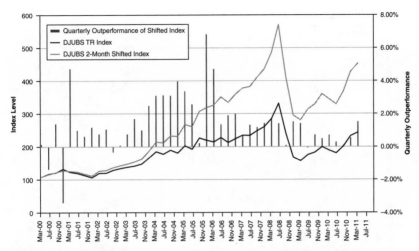

Exhibit 13-1   Total Returns of DJUBS Two-Month Shifted Index Relative to the Standard DJUBSCI

Source: Bloomberg, PIMCO, as of March 31, 2011

commodity indexes attempt to harvest, it is important that commodity indexes become increasingly diversified across their roll period and contract tenors as the amount of assets invested in them grows. More recently developed commodity indexes, such as the CSCB, incorporate these ideas by rolling over a 15-day window and holding contracts that cover the first three listed months. This idea of holding multiple contracts can be extended even further to all contracts across the curve of each commodity. It seems the most scalable solution for index investors to avoid distortions in the market is to weight the holdings of each contract across the curve by their relative open interest. (Such an approach is currently employed by J.P. Morgan in its Commodity Curve Index [CCI].) This approach is theoretically very attractive because it matches the index's liquidity requirements with the activity in the market. However, implementation of this approach involves holding a large number of contracts across many different commodities, making implementation potentially overwhelming.

While all these different approaches for determining which contract to hold might appear different on the surface, they are

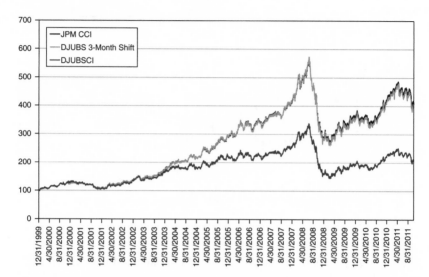

Exhibit 13-2 JPM Comodity Curve Index Returns Relative to the DJUBS Three-Month Shifted Index and the Regular DJUBSCI

Source: Bloomberg, as of September 30, 2011

basically identical to holding a given shifted index. Exhibit 13-2 shows the JPM index that holds dozens of contracts across the commodity curve relative to the DJUBS three-month shifted index and the regular DJUBSCI (we have normalized commodity weights for each index to remove this source of variation, thereby isolating the variation due to curve positioning and roll dates). The DJUBS three-month shifted index rolls over five days and just holds one contract (per commodity) three months out the curve. The JPM CCI holds anywhere from several to a few dozen contracts (per commodity) and rolls over 10 days. In the end, the results show that the diversification benefits of being spread out across the curve of each commodity are often overstated. Just simply moving the commodity exposure three months out the curve has been sufficient to perfectly replicate exposure held along the curve in a large number of different contracts! This highlights how efficient the market is in pricing the various commodity curves once the level of risk premium in the very front contracts has been accounted for. It also emphasizes the importance for investors in maximizing the risk premium if they are to maximize their long-term returns.

While much work has been focused to date on altering the positioning on the curve or the days over which the index roll occurs, the underlying goal has typically been to reduce the liquidity footprint of the index. However, whether you change the roll dates or the contracts that are held, the improvement in performance is a function of capturing the distortions in the risk premium at the very front of the curve, just as in the previous example. As such, we believe there has been more than sufficient analysis within this vein, but there has been far too little work done on addressing the issue of which commodities an investor should hold. Perhaps the 20 commodities held in the DJUBSCI or the 24 commodities held in the S&P GSCI are too many.

PICKING THE RIGHT COMMODITIES AND THEIR WEIGHTS

We believe future commodity indexes should focus less on providing just a measure of the daily performance of a large basket of futures and more on adding long-term value to investors by generating the highest level of long-term excess returns while preserving the diversification and inflation-hedging characteristics of the commodity asset class.

The standard commodity indexes today set weights based upon some function of liquidity or global production. This historic style of index creation—including in the index a large number of commodities and picking weights based on global production or some other quantity or value factor—is very similar to the way that equity indexes are constructed. The S&P 500 is constructed and weighted based upon market capitalization of the companies that make up the index. That style of construction may work fine for equity investors who want broad exposure to the market and believe that the market is efficient enough so they have little reason to expect the shares of one company to outperform the shares of another company. However, in commodity markets the playing field is not as level. There is a reason why certain commodities can be expected a priori to outperform other commodities. A great deal of information about the future return of investing in commodities can be anticipated by looking at the storage costs and the historic levels of risk premium across various commodities (see Chapter 6, "Maximizing Roll Yield"). To date, commodity indexes have ignored this most basic but unique feature of commodity markets.

Moreover, an index should focus on obtaining broad exposure to the various commodity sectors (grains, energies, metals, etc.), with emphasis on the diversification among commodity sectors, rather than being an all-inclusive set of every commodity that passes some liquidity test. Again, the commodity markets are different from the equity markets in this respect. In equities, there is a common equity beta factor that is quite strong across the various sectors. Some sectors like healthcare might be low beta, while others like technology are high beta; but for most individual names and sectors, the underlying correlation to one another is reasonably high. Commodities are unique from equities in this respect because the correlation across different commodity sectors is very low. There is no long-term common factor linking the gold market to the oil and corn markets, as there is in the equity market. (In the short term, flows into commodity indexes or low real interest rates may temporarily raise correlations across commodities, but these are often temporary increases in correlation.) Understanding and exploiting this basic factor is essential to building a truly diversified commodity index.

How much diversification is really achieved by owning both heating oil and crude oil or both soybeans and corn? To help shed light on this question, Exhibit 13-3 shows the correlation matrix for the daily returns of eight different commodities. Two commodities were selected from four different commodity sectors, namely, Brent crude and heating oil for energy, gold and silver for precious metals, copper and aluminum for base metals, and corn and soybeans

	Brent Crude	Heating Oil	Gold	Silver	Copper	Aluminum	Corn	Soybeans
Brent Crude	100%	89%	26%	29%	33%	28%	26%	28%
Heating Oil	89%	100%	24%	25%	28%	25%	22%	25%
Gold	26%	24%	100%	75%	32%	27%	19%	19%
Silver	29%	25%	75%	100%	40%	35%	24%	26%
Copper	33%	28%	32%	40%	100%	72%	24%	27%
Aluminum	28%	25%	27%	35%	72%	100%	22%	24%
Corn	26%	22%	19%	24%	24%	22%	100%	65%
Soybeans	28%	25%	19%	26%	27%	24%	65%	100%

Exhibit 13-3 **Correlation Matrix for the Daily Returns of Select Commodities**

Source: Bloomberg, PIMCO, as of June 30, 2011

for agricultural products. Notice that the correlations between the commodities within the same sectors are very high, while the correlations between commodities from different sectors are quite low. In the case of energy, the correlation between Brent crude and heating oil is 89%. There is very little diversification benefit achieved from holding both Brent crude oil and heating oil in a commodity index. This doesn't mean that an index shouldn't hold both commodities if liquidity or other factors suggest that holding both is advantageous, but the reason for holding both Brent crude oil and heating oil should not be related to providing increased diversification.

Outside the energy sector, the highest correlation between Brent crude oil and any of the other commodities shown is with copper at 33%. The same type of relation exists across the other sectors of base metals, precious metals, and grains. For example, the correlation between gold and silver is 75%, but outside precious metals, the next highest correlation is with copper at 32%. The primary driver of diversification is the number of unique commodity sectors that are included. The number of commodities in an index has a second-order impact on diversification. Therefore, the real benefits of diversification come, not from owning dozens of different commodities, but rather from owning several different commodity sectors, such as grains, energy, livestock, base metals, precious metals, and softs.

This conclusion is important because it means that if a particular commodity, such as corn, has high storage costs relative to another grain, such as soybeans, then the corn exposure may be replaced by soybean exposure. Such a substitution allows an investor to improve the return expectations of the commodity index without diminishing the expected diversification benefits.

In addition to long-term return potential and correlation, the level of volatility of individual commodities should also be considered in deciding both the sector and individual commodity weights. Ultimately, sector and individual commodity weights should be driven by a combination of liquidity, volatility, correlation, and return expectations of each commodity and sector. Such an approach will assure a more optimal balancing of risk and return than the standard existing commodity indexes.

PICKING THE RIGHT COLLATERAL

So far, the focus on enhancing commodity index returns has centered on improving returns on the commodities portion of the index. However, the commodity futures must be backed by collateral, and this collateral can be managed in many different ways. Currently all commodity indexes assume that the futures are backed by three-month Treasury bills. Treasury bills are arguably the safest, most liquid financial asset. Therefore, they should be expected to have a long-run return below other financial assets.

In general, LIBOR is the assumed financing rate embedded in financial transactions such as futures. For example, the spread between different contract months of S&P equity futures is a function of the level of LIBOR. LIBOR is also the financing rate assumed in calculating the full carry or spread between commodity futures. LIBOR is the rate that must be earned on collateral if an investor seeks to offset the implied financing rate embedded in the futures markets. From 2000 to 2011, the average spread between three-month Treasury bills and three-month LIBOR has been 48 bps. In addition to moving from T-bills to enhanced cash collateral that can likely earn LIBOR plus some incremental spread, there are other options that investors might consider. For investors looking to commodities as a means of inflation protection, using TIPS as the collateral to back commodity futures may provide a more complete inflation hedge since the return on collateral is explicitly linked to the rate of inflation. In general, the selection of collateral should be consistent with an investor's risk and return objectives, but moving out of T-bills and into some other form of collateral will often provide enhanced returns. In addition to better returns, moving from T-bills to another type of collateral can also improve the diversification or inflation-hedging properties of a commodity investment.

THE FEWER COMMODITY, LOW-STORAGE-COST, ENHANCED-COLLATERAL COMMODITY INDEX: A NEW INDEX CONCEPT FROM PIMCO

With knowledge of storage costs across the various individual commodities, it is possible to estimate in advance which commodities an optimized roll yield strategy is most likely to hold on average. Before going into details for the construction of a static storage cost–based portfolio, it is worth highlighting the main difference between this approach to maximizing roll yield and the more dynamic "optimized" roll yield approaches discussed in Chapter 6. Since the storage cost approach is static, it should be viewed more as an index rather than a strategy. The purpose of an index is to serve as a reference or guide to the relative movement of a basket of assets. It is supposed to be a yardstick that allows an investor to understand at a high level how different asset classes perform relative to one another across time. In order to be as useful as possible as a historic reference, the constituents that make up the index should change as little as possible across time. In addition, the general underlying components of the index should be easily understood and observed both ex-ante and ex-post. Due to the dynamic nature of the optimized roll yield strategies, these conditions are not met. There are months when an optimized roll yield strategy has zero agriculture exposure, and there are other months where it has over 40% exposure to agricultural commodities. Such volatility of weights means it is not useful as a broad measure of the commodity asset class. This does not suggest that it is a bad strategy or that it will fail to successfully generate long-term returns, but it is important to remember that it is a trading strategy that shifts from one commodity to the other and back again and not an accurate measure of the performance of the commodity asset class.

In order to be both diversified and broadly representative of the commodity asset class, the low-storage-cost index is constructed to have exposure to each of five major commodity sectors, namely, agriculture, energy, precious metals, base metals, and meats. In each of those five sectors, the index goes long the commodity with the lowest storage cost. In the case of agriculture, it is soybeans that have the lowest storage cost, crude oil in the case of energy, gold in the case of precious metals, and nickel in the case of base metals.

In practice, optimal weights for each commodity and sector could be set based upon a combination of some measure of forward-looking return expectations, historical correlations and volatility, liquidity, and global production. Alternatively, if tracking error to published indexes is a concern, the sector weights of the low-storage-cost index could be set to match the sector weights of any major index, such as the DJUBSCI or S&P GSCI. However, in this example, we set the weights of the low-storage-cost index equal to the average sector weights of the optimized roll yield strategy discussed in Chapter 6. We do this to ensure as much of an apples-to-apples comparison as possible between the two strategies. In addition, since the storage costs of meats are difficult to assess, the commodities in this sector were held in the same average weights as in the optimized roll yield strategy to make the comparison as close as possible. Finally, in energy the allocation was split evenly between Brent and WTI crude oil for the low-storage-cost index.

In addition to making the commodity selection more thoughtful by looking at storage costs and expected future returns, the collateral backing is assumed to earn the return of the current three-month LIBOR rate. As previously discussed, this is the assumed financing rate underlying most financial transactions, and it is a better measure of the return that investors should expect on their capital than Treasury bills.

Exhibits 13-4 and 13-5 show the performance of the low-storage-cost index relative to the previously discussed optimal roll yield strategy since 2000. Overall, the best total returns were found in the low-storage-cost index. The main driver for this was the improved spot returns of the low-storage-cost index. As previously discussed in Chapter 6, this was expected since the low-storage-cost index is static in nature. While the roll yield of the low-storage-cost index is not as high as the optimized roll yield strategy, this is more than offset by the improved spot returns. The low-storage-cost index also benefited from a marginally higher return on collateral than the optimized roll yield index because the three-month LIBOR was on average nearly 50 bps higher than three-month Treasury bills. Furthermore, this analysis ignores any impact of transaction costs or slippage in execution, which would be significantly higher for the optimized roll yield strategy.

	EW Index	Top Half Roll Yield Index, (Optimized Roll Yield Strategy)	Bottom Half Roll Yield Index	Low-Storage-Cost Index
Total Return	10.25%	15.13%	5.37%	16.68%
Excess Return	7.73%	12.61%	2.85%	13.66%
Roll Yield Return	−7.73%	5.42%	20.87%	−1.57%
Spot Return	15.46%	7.20%	23.72%	15.23%

Exhibit 13-4 **Returns Analysis for Equal Weights Index, Low-Storage-Cost Index, as well as Indexes That Consist of Commodities with the Best and Worst Roll Yields, Respectively**

Source: PIMCO, Bloomberg, as of December 31, 2010

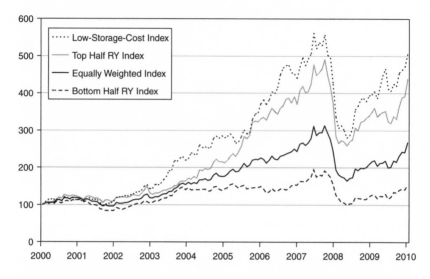

Exhibit 13-5 Total Return for Equally Weighted Index, Low-Storage-Cost Index, as well as Indexes That Consist of Commodities with the Best and Worst Roll Yields, Respectively

Source: PIMCO, Bloomberg, as of December 31, 2010

But the real virtue of the low-storage-cost approach is in its simplicity. The fact that it performed better than the optimized roll yield strategy is nice, but the real comparison is also versus the equally weighted index. The low-storage-cost index and the equally weighted index had nearly identical spot returns, meaning that they both accurately captured the changes in spot prices of commodities over this period. However, the better total returns of the low-storage-cost index were achieved not by any fancy trading strategy but merely by lowering the storage costs that the index investor paid (and also selecting a more sensible source of collateral backing).

It is worthwhile to step back and consider what it means to buy and roll a long-only basket of commodity futures in order to understand why the low-storage-cost index works as well as it does. When investors go long a commodity futures contract, they have fixed the price for a future purchase of a commodity. Index investors who own a whole basket of futures and roll them forward are effectively buying and rolling forward their future ownership of that basket of physical commodities. In essence, commodity index investors are very similar to operators of a warehouse. Both index investors and warehouse operators have purchased some items with the hope of selling them later for a profit. In order for warehouse operators to make a profit, they must buy things that can be resold later at a price high enough to offset storage and operating costs. If the warehouse operators have no view about the relative price outlook for two similar items, they should buy the one that is the least costly to store.

This is the same position in which index investors find themselves. They are operating a hypothetical warehouse where they get paid the convenience yield and price appreciation, and the cost to the index investors is the actual storage plus financing costs. For index investors who want exposure to a broad basket of commodities, the default position should be to own a basket of commodities that cost the least to store. Understanding the impact and importance of storage costs does not mean that investors should never own commodities with high storage costs. Deviations can be made from the default low-storage-cost portfolio, but they should be made tactically based upon supply and demand fundamentals in light of the long-term headwinds of such a position. The purpose of utilizing an index that consists of a basket of low-storage-cost commodities is twofold: it provides a transparent measure of the asset class, and given its structural long-term advantage, it is a useful passive measure to accurately judge the value provided by different managers, trading strategies, and rules-based enhancements.

CONCLUSION

After starting with the history of commodity indexing, we have spent the bulk of this book discussing better and smarter ways to obtain systematic, long-only exposure to this very important asset class. In this chapter, we have shared some thoughts on the future of commodity index investing, ending with an example of what such an index might look like.

Conclusion

As we said in our Introduction, we wanted to:

- Define precisely what is meant by the term "commodity indexes"
- Explain the drivers of return to the asset class and show how commodities can contribute to diversification and inflation hedging
- Describe strategies that an intelligent commodity index investor can use to attempt to achieve returns that are more attractive than a simple calculated index
- Discuss the important issues of portfolio management and risk management
- Provide a look to the future of commodity index investing

We have tried to describe strategies and investment approaches that can actually be used by investors who allocate to this asset class.

Commodity futures for investment, as measured by an investable index, have a fairly short history but a robust following. Investors are using this asset class to seek acceptable returns that might be expected also to provide inflation protection and diversification from stocks and bonds in their portfolios. There are economic reasons, based on the drivers of returns, for investors to look for those benefits.

The variety, complexity, and sophistication of commodity indexes have increased along with investor interest in the asset class. But an intelligent commodity index investor is not satisfied with simply achieving the passive returns of an index, no matter how sophisticated. There are several ways to add value to an index, without losing the key benefits that led the investor to the asset class in the first place:

- There are strategies that can capitalize on the roll yield—an integral consideration in index implementation—affecting when to roll positions and which contracts to roll into.
- There are strategies that recognize the seasonal nature of many commodity markets.
- There are strategies that recognize opportunities to hold positions in markets other than the market used to calculate an index.
- There are strategies that can take advantage of mispriced volatility, especially if the investor understands the reason that volatility might be mispriced.
- There are strategies to manage effectively the collateral that is an integral part of commodity index investing.
- There are risk and implementation considerations that must be clearly understood.

Besides taking advantage of these many opportunities to add value, intelligent index investors will understand the need to incorporate a diversified set of these enhancement strategies in their portfolio, rather than relying on any single approach. They will understand that the commodity markets, both cash and futures, are dynamic, so that any static approach may be suboptimal. These investors further understand the important need to control risk in their commodity index portfolio—the risk associated with any single strategy as well as the total portfolio risk. We have described how investors may approach that risk.

Finally, any commodity index strategy inherently includes investment in the fixed income that collateralizes commodity positions. Intelligent choice of that collateral as well as active management of that collateral also may add value to the total commodity portfolio.

Commodity index investing should be viewed, not in isolation, but within the context of an investor's total portfolio. This asset class will continue to play an increasingly important role in those portfolios. This book was designed to help our readers take advantage of the asset class more intelligently, while learning more about the benefits that commodity indexes offer. We hope that you have gained insight from this book and that you have enjoyed reading it as much as we have enjoyed writing it.

References

Ankrim, Ernest M., and Chris R. Hensel. 1993. "Commodities in Asset Allocation: A Real-Asset Alternative to Real Estate." *Financial Analysts Journal*, vol. 49, no. 3 (May/June):20–29.

De Chiara, Adam, and Daniel M. Raab. 2002. "The Benefits of Real Asset Portfolio Diversification." AIG Trading Group.

Erb, Claude B., and Campbell R. Harvey. 2006. "The Tactical and Strategic Value of Commodity Futures." *Financial Analysts Journal*, vol. 62, no. 2 (March/April):69–97.

Fernholz, Robert, and Brian Shay. 1982. "Stochastic Portfolio Theory and Stock Market Equilibrium." *Journal of Finance*, vol. 37, no. 2 (May):615–624.

Gorton, Gary, and K. Geert Rouwenhorst. 2006. "Facts and Fantasies About Commodity Futures." *Financial Analysts Journal*, vol. 62, no. 2 (March/April):47–68.

Greer, Robert J. 1978. "Conservative Commodities: A Key Inflation Hedge." *Journal of Portfolio Management*, vol. 4, no. 4 (Summer):26–29.

———. 1997. "What Is an Asset Class, Anyway?" *Journal of Portfolio Management*, vol. 23, no. 2 (Winter):86–91.

———. 2000. "The Nature of Commodity Index Returns." *Journal of Alternative Investments* (Summer):45–53.

Kaldor, Nicholas. 1939. "Speculation and Economic Stability." *Review of Economic Studies*, vol. 7, no. 1 (October):1–27.

Keynes, John Maynard. 1930. *Treatise on Money*. London: Macmillan.

Working, Holbrook. 1949. "The Theory of Price of Storage." *American Economic Review*, vol. 39, no. 6 (December):1254–1262.

Index

About the Authors

 **Robert J. Greer** first entered commodity markets 40 years ago, following graduation from the Stanford Business School. This inspired him to design what is considered the world's first investable commodity index. He continued his career with inflation assets (commercial real estate) before returning to commodities in the 1990s, managing commodity index products. At PIMCO since 2002, he partnered with his coauthors to build a robust real return business.

 **Nic Johnson** manages several commodity portfolios at PIMCO, including the Commodities Plus Strategy, developing and applying the fundamental insights as well as the quantitative strategies presented in this book. Nic has a master's degree in financial mathematics from the University of Chicago and formerly was a true "rocket scientist," working at NASA's Jet Propulsion Lab. When not working, Nic enjoys spending time with his wife and their two boys.

 **Mihir P. Worah** is the head of the real return practice at PIMCO, responsible for over $100 billion in dedicated actively managed inflation hedging strategies. He manages the PIMCO Commodity RealReturn Strategy, which served as a crucible for the development of many of the ideas presented in this book. He has a PhD in theoretical physics from the University of Chicago and enjoys playing the guitar with his son.